Study Guide for Book Clubs: The Overstory

KATHRYN COPE

CONTENTS

INTRODUCTION

There are few things more rewarding than getting together with a group of like-minded people and discussing a good book. Book club meetings, at their best, are vibrant, passionate affairs. Each member will bring along a different perspective and ideally there will be heated debate.

A surprising number of book club members, however, report that their meetings have been a disappointment. Even though their group loved the particular book they were discussing, they could think of astonishingly little to say about it. Failing to find interesting discussion angles for a book is the single most common reason for book group discussions to fall flat. Most book groups only meet once a month and a lackluster meeting is frustrating for everyone.

Study Guides for Book Clubs were born out of a passion for reading groups. Packed with information, they take the hard work out of preparing for a meeting and ensure that your book group discussions never run dry. How you choose to use the guides is entirely up to you. The author biography, context, and style sections provide useful background information which may be interesting to share with your group at the beginning of your meeting. The all-important list of discussion questions, which will probably form the core of your meeting, can be found towards the end of this guide. To support your responses to the discussion questions, you may find it helpful to refer to the "Themes" and "Character" sections.

A detailed plot synopsis is provided as an aide-memoire if you need to recap on the finer points of the plot. There is also a quick quiz—a fun way to test your knowledge and bring your discussion to a close. Finally, if this was a book that you particularly enjoyed, the guide concludes with a list of books similar in style or subject matter.

This guide contains spoilers. Please do not be tempted to read it before you have read the original novel as plot surprises will be well and truly ruined.

Kathryn Cope, 2019

RICHARD POWERS

When Richard Powers was awarded the 2019 Pulitzer Prize for Fiction for *The Overstory*, it marked the fruition of an already distinguished career as a novelist. For the past thirty years, Powers has produced a steady stream of novels, been the recipient of the prestigious MacArthur grant (awarded for creative "genius") and received numerous accolades. With this in mind, many readers may wonder why they have only just come across his work.

The key to Powers's low profile seems to lie in the ability of his novels to divide critics (a quality which also makes them perfect book club material). Many reviewers feel that the genius of Powers's work has been woefully overlooked by the reading public. Others believe that his focus upon cerebral concepts over characterization has prevented many readers from warming to him. Every one of his books tackles complex ideas (often science-related), from genetic engineering to virtual reality. While some readers welcome the challenge of his ambitious scope, others find it off-putting. This polarity of views raises interesting questions about what the purpose of fiction should be. Is it to entertain or inform? Should it confirm our own vision of ourselves, or challenge our perception of the world? When addressed with these questions, Powers is vocal and unapologetic in his beliefs. At a time when "human activity is unraveling the climate," he is adamant that literary fiction needs to do more than focus on the psychological conflicts of individual characters.

The impressive intellectual scope of Powers's work is reflected in his background. Born in 1957 in Illinois, his family relocated, first to North Chicago and then to Bangkok, Thailand. From childhood he had a broad range of interests. A versatile musician (playing the cello, guitar, clarinet and saxophone), he also developed an early interest in science and literature. At university he chose to study physics believing that he was "destined" to become a scientist. Once he realized that a career in science would limit him to a narrow specialization, however, he transferred to a course in literature. In 1980 he changed intellectual direction again, working as a computer programmer in Boston. Here, a visit to the Museum of Fine Arts changed his life. Inspired by a black-and-white photograph of three farm boys on their way to a dance, he gave up his job to write a novel. The resulting *Three Farmers on Their Way to a Dance* was published in 1985 and met with critical success. From that point, he produced a new novel every two to three years, each of them addressing a completely different field of research—from Disney and nuclear warfare in *Prisoner's Dilemma* (1988) to biohacking in *Orfeo* (2014).

Given Powers's fascination with the impact of science and progress, it seems inevitable that he turned to the hot topic of environmental destruction for his twelfth novel, *The Overstory*. Like all of his novels, the book is based on an intellectual engagement with his topic and meticulous research (Powers read over one hundred books on trees while writing it). Its seeds, however, were sewn by the emotional experience of a tree epiphany. While teaching at Stanford University, Powers saw his first Californian redwood and realized that, until that moment, he had been "tree blind." As well as inspiring his writing, the encounter prompted the author to move from his home in Palo Alto to a secluded cabin in the Smokey Mountains.

CONTEXT

Redwood Summer

Much of *The Overstory*'s plot is inspired by events that took place during the Redwood Summer of 1990. Over a three-month period, the environmental group Earth First! protested against the logging of Californian redwoods by timber companies. Powers sets his novel during the same time period and the actions taken by Olivia, Nick, Douglas and Mimi have many parallels with the actions of Earth First!

The activist activities of Redwood Summer were prompted by two incidents which spelled trouble for what remained of California's old-growth redwoods. The first was a proposed change in legislation known as California Proposition 130. While Earth First! hoped this law to restrict logging would be passed (in the end it was not), its members also foresaw that logging companies would anticipate this by accelerating their logging rates while they still could. The second factor, was the takeover of the Pacific Lumber Company (one of California's largest timber companies) by Maxxam Inc. First established in 1863, the Pacific Lumber Company was a family business that had maintained a sustainable growth policy until it was taken over by Texan financier Charles Hurwitz. Once his corporation, Maxxam Inc., took control, sustainability was replaced by the policy of clearcutting for a quick profit. This scenario is reflected in *The Overstory* when the leader of the Life Defense Force, Mother N, explains to new recruits that Humboldt Timber was a family business with a sustainable cutting policy until a hostile takeover (incidentally, the Pacific Lumber Company is now called Humboldt Redwood Company).

Before the public protests of Redwood Summer even began, Earth First! made headlines when two of its members were involved in an explosion. Judi Bari (the group's leader) and Darryl Cherney were on their way to an Earth First! event when a bomb under the driver's seat exploded. Both survived but were badly injured—Judi Bari more so, suffering a fractured pelvis. Soon afterwards, Bari and Cherney were accused by the FBI of transporting explosives with the intent to carry out an act of eco-terrorism. Both denied any knowledge that the explosives were in the car and claimed that they had received recent death threats. The case went to court and the couple was found not guilty due to a lack of evidence to back up the FBI's claims. Bari and Cherney sued the FBI and, twelve years later, a jury concluded that the FBI had violated the activists' rights and defamed their characters. Cherney and Bari were awarded $4.4 million but by this time Judi Bari had died of cancer. This incident clearly inspired the death of Mother N in *The Overstory*. Despite Mother N's commitment to pacifism, the police insist that she was responsible for the explosion in which she died, claiming that she was planning an act of eco-terrorism.

During Redwood Summer, Earth First! used symbolic protest to deliver its message. Like the activists in *The Overstory*, members dressed in animal costumes and camouflaged themselves as trees. They also attempted to disrupt the logging industry in a variety of ways. Tactics often involved physical obstruction where activists placed their bodies in the way of felling—chaining themselves to trees or bulldozers, blocking the path of trucks, and tree-sitting. More controversially, they also disarmed machinery and, at least in the early days, spiked trees. The aim of tree spiking (inserting a metal spike into a tree trunk) was to make it difficult for loggers to cut down trees without damaging their equipment. The tactic became controversial after a sawmill worker was badly injured when the bandsaw he was using shattered after hitting a hidden spike in a piece of wood. Keen to stress that they were a non-violent organization (although there has been some debate over how radical their methods were), Earth First! announced that they would no longer use tree spiking as part of their campaign.

Julia "Butterfly" Hill

The character of Olivia Vandergriff bears a strong resemblance to Julia "Butterfly" Hill—an environmental activist who took tree-sitting to a whole new level. Like Olivia, Hill experienced a dramatic life-changing moment which set her on a spiritual quest. In Hill's case, this was a near-fatal car accident in which she was hit by a drunk driver. At the age of twenty-two, she had to learn to walk and talk again and reassessed her life, realizing that, instead of pursuing money and success, she wanted to make a positive contribution to the world.

Hill found her cause when she learned about the logging of redwood trees in Humboldt County, California. Seeking out the activists who were protesting there, she volunteered to tree-sit a 180-foot Californian redwood, estimated to be about 1500 years old. Hill ascended the tree, known as Luna, on December 10, 1997 with initial plans to stay up there for a week. In the end, she remained there for 738 days. On December 18, 1999, she finally vacated the tree when the Pacific Lumber Company agreed to preserve Luna, along with all other trees within a 200-foot area.

While residing in Luna, Hill slept on a platform in a sleeping bag and withstood 40 mph winds, harassment by helicopter and abuse from loggers. At the same time, she conducted interviews for radio and TV to gain publicity for the campaign. Passionate and eloquent when interviewed, Hill was also photogenic (improbably so given her living conditions) and became the unofficial poster girl for the environmental movement. Her allure was so great that one of the loggers she was obstructing fell in love with her and consequently gave up his job with Pacific Lumber.

David Chain

At one point in *The Overstory*, Powers depicts Mimi and Douglas taking part in a peaceful protest. This protest descends into unexpected carnage when loggers begin to fell trees, regardless of the protesters who have chained themselves to trees and logging equipment. This scene may have been inspired by the death of David Chain, an Earth First! activist. In 1998 Chain died instantly from a head injury when he was struck by a 135-foot falling tree on Pacific Lumber property. The timber company claimed that loggers were unaware of the presence of protesters. Members of Earth First!, however, said that the loggers had been deliberately felling trees in their direction. In the aftermath of her son's death, Chain's mother filed a civil suit against Pacific Lumber. Three days before the trial was due to begin, she accepted a wrongful death settlement for an undisclosed sum. As part of this settlement it was agreed that the tree that had killed Chain would remain where it had fallen, and logging would be prohibited in the 100-foot zone surrounding it.

Suzanne Simard

Richard Powers has specified that the work of Dr Suzanne Simard provided much of the inspiration for Patricia Westerford's research in his novel. A Canadian professor of Forest and Conservation Sciences, Simard has undertaken ground-breaking work on the underground networks of forests and the way trees communicate through a "wood wide web." Her research in this area has led to mainstream recognition of tree communication skills.

Vandana Shiva

Further inspiration for Patricia Westerford's work seems to have come from Vandana Shiva, an Indian environmental activist and author. Born in 1952, Shiva has devoted her life to promoting and preserving biodiversity and has campaigned against the use of harmful pesticides. She is best known, however, for promoting "seed freedom" and founding the largest seed bank in India. The scheme encourages villagers to give indigenous seeds to the seed bank to preserve biodiversity.

Shiva developed the idea of seed freedom in direct opposition to the World Trade Organization's 1994 Trade Related Intellectual Property Rights agreement—an agreement which enables corporations to apply for patents on seeds. Condemning this process as "biopiracy," Shiva has questioned the ethics of claiming legal ownership of living things (a recurring theme in *The Overstory*). Her campaigning has involved fighting against the attempts of several large corporations to claim ownership over indigenous Indian seeds. In 2001, for example, she successfully prevented the US company, RiceTec from acquiring a patent on basmati rice.

The Chipko Movement

As a student, Vandana Shiva was a member of the Chipko movement—an Indian forest conservation group that emerged in the 1970s. In *The Overstory*, Mother N refers to the courage of the Chipko women in a rousing speech.

From the 1960s onwards, the heavily forested Himalayan regions of India became a magnet for foreign logging companies. Meanwhile, poor rural villagers, who depended on the forests for food and fuel were prohibited from managing the forests by the government. Clearcutting undertaken by the logging companies soon led to poor soil quality in the area (impacting agriculture), a scarcity of water, and land erosion. The commercial felling of large areas of forest significantly contributed to the catastrophic flooding of the Alaknanda River in the Chamoli district of Uttarakhand in July 1970.

When, in 1974, the government auctioned off an area of forest close to the Alaknanda River, the villagers of nearby Reni protested. The government sold the land regardless and, on the day a lumber crew were scheduled to cut down the trees, the men of Reni were invited to a meeting to discuss compensation—a ruse to keep them out of the way. When the lumber crew arrived at the site near Reni, however, they were confronted by the women of the village. Despite being threatened with guns, the women protected the trees from being felled by hugging them. It is from these actions that the group gained its name (*chipko* is the Hindi word for "hug" or "cling to"). The women maintained their position all night and, when the male villagers returned the next day, they added to their numbers. Word spread to nearby villagers and more people came to join the protest. After four days, the timber contractors gave up and left.

When news of the protest reached state ministers, a committee was created to investigate the effects of deforestation. The results were unexpected and unprecedented in Indian history. The state ruled in favour of the villagers and imposed a ten-year ban on commercial logging in the area. From this point, the Chipko movement spread across the Indian Himalayas, as more and more villagers joined the fight against large-scale commercial deforestation. The successful, non-violent resistance of the Chipko movement inspired environmental action groups all over the world.

Wangari Maathai

In Patricia Westerford's speeches she cites Wangari Maathai as an eco-heroine. Born in Kenya in 1940, Professor Maathai was the first woman in East and Central Africa to earn a doctorate. She devoted herself to the dual goals of empowering Kenyan women and conserving the environment. In 1977 she established the Green Belt Movement. The organization's aim was to demonstrate to women in rural Kenya that planting trees could not only combat deforestation but also improve their quality of life, providing fuel and sustainable income. Maathai was awarded the Nobel Peace Prize in 2004. She died in 2011 but her work continues through the Green Belt Movement. As a result of the scheme, over 30,000 women have been trained in forestry and over 50 million trees have been planted.

Chico Mendes

Another of Patricia's environmental heroes is Francisco Alves Mendes Filho, otherwise known as Chico Mendes. Born in 1944, Mendes was a Brazilian rubber tapper (a traditional, sustainable process by which latex is removed from a rubber tree without harming it).

By the 1970s, the livelihoods of Brazilian rubber tappers were increasingly at risk, as rubber tree forests were sold off to quick profit logging companies. Gaining the support of his fellow rubber workers, Mendes petitioned the government to establish Amazon rainforest reserves. He also led blockades to obstruct deforestation, standing in front of chainsaws, tractors and other logging machinery. The success of Mendes's campaigning made him unpopular with would-be developers. In 1988 he was murdered by the son of Darly Alves da Silva—a rancher whose commercial plans had been foiled by Mendes.

Occupy Wall Street

In *The Overstory*, Powers describes Adam walking through Zuccotti Park in Manhattan in 2011. Here he witnesses hundreds of activists camped out in tents and sleeping bags in the Occupy Wall Street protest.

Occupy Wall Street was essentially a protest against capitalism and greed. Protesters took over the financial district of New York City to make their point. The movement combined concern over the environmental impact of rampant consumerism with outrage over the gap between the richest and poorest in society.

The Stanford Prison Experiment

At the beginning of Douglas's narrative in *The Overstory*, he takes part in the Stanford Prison Experiment. This was a psychological experiment that took place at Stanford University in 1971. Funded by the U.S. Office of Naval Research, the aim of the study was ostensibly to analyze causes of conflict between guards and prisoners. The psychologists conducting the experiment, however, were interested in the wider question of how perceived power and group identity would impact on the behaviour of the participants.

Douglas's experiences accurately reflect the process that participants in the experiment went through. Twenty-four young men (all white and middle-class) were selected to take part on the understanding that they would be paid $15 per day. Half of them were allocated the roles of guards, while the other half would be prisoners within a simulated prison environment.

The men who were to be prisoners soon realized that they had drawn the short straw. Without warning, they were arrested, processed at a police station, blindfolded, and taken to "Stanford County Jail'" (a basement at Stanford University made to look like a prison). Here they were searched, stripped naked and doused with delousing spray before being issued with a uniform and a heavy ankle chain. On the back of each uniform was a prison ID number. Guards received a briefing from Philip Zimbardo, the psychologist in charge of the experiment. Issuing the guards with batons, Zimbardo instructed them to undermine the prisoners' individuality by referring to them only by their number and generally treating them with disrespect. Prisoners were housed in cramped cells with nothing but a bed while guards had access to comfortable areas and other luxuries.

From the second day of the experiment there was conflict between prisoners and guards. A mini riot took place where some of the prisoners blockaded their cell door and refused to obey the guards' instructions. In response, the guards attacked the prisoners with fire extinguishers and established a "privilege cell" where prisoners who had not been involved in the rebellion could enjoy rewards. After only thirty-five hours, one prisoner had to be removed from the experiment when he descended into a state of frenzied rage and distress. Some of the guards, meanwhile, imposed increasingly sadistic punishments. Sanitation buckets were left unemptied, leading to increasingly unsanitary conditions. Mattresses were removed, forcing prisoners to sleep on concrete floors, and prisoners were humiliated by being made to strip.

Most of the prisoners passively accepted the abuse doled out by the guards and, at the encouragement of their jailors, even turned on those prisoners who rebelled. One such rebel was Prisoner 416 who declared that he was on hunger strike in protest against the behaviour of the guards. In response, the guards transferred him to "solitary confinement" (a dark closet). The other prisoners were informed that Prisoner 416 would be released if they gave up their blankets for the night. Only one prisoner volunteered to do so.

Although the experiment was scheduled to last for two weeks, Philip Zimbardo aborted it after only six days when his girlfriend (a graduate psychology student) interviewed the participants and questioned the ethics of the experiment. Most of the guards were reportedly disappointed at this early end to the experience.

In the aftermath of the Stanford Prison Experiment its purpose, methodology and ethics have been debated. The project's critics have pointed out that it was not a true experiment at all, as it did not lead to any meaningful results or conclusions. Many have also questioned the morality of placing young men in this potentially traumatizing situation—particularly as Zimbardo did not allow participants to withdraw from the experiment when they expressed a wish to do so.

PLOT SYNOPSIS

ROOTS

Nicholas Hoel

During chestnut season in mid-nineteenth-century Brooklyn, Jørgen Hoel (a Norwegian immigrant) meets Irish girl, Vi Powys. They marry and move to Iowa where the government is giving away land to those prepared to farm it. On their land Jørgen plants the six chestnuts he had in his pocket on the day he proposed to his wife. Although chestnuts are not native to the area, the saplings grow. Over the years, five of them die but one remains.

As Jørgen and Vi grow old, their eldest son John takes over the running of the farm. As the twentieth century begins, he takes advantage of progress and buys a steam tractor. Vi dies and, bedridden, Jørgen looks out on the leaves of the tree he planted.

When Jørgen dies, John buries his father beneath the chestnut. By this time the "Hoel Chestnut" has become a local landmark and the farm is prosperous. Buying a camera, John decides to take a photograph of the tree on the 21st day of every month. By 1904, unbeknown to John, a disease (spread from an imported Chinese chestnut) begins decimating the chestnut population in New York. Soon it spreads as far as New England.

John dies and the farm passes to his two sons, Carl and Frank. Frank continues his father's photographic project. When Frank goes off to fight in World War I, his son Frank Jr, promises to carry on photographing the chestnut tree. He continues to keep this promise after Frank Sr is killed in action.

Blight continues to devastate chestnut trees across the USA. By 1940, four billion have died. The only survivors are those planted by pioneers, miles away from their native territory.

By World War II five hundred photographs of the Hoel

Chestnut have been taken. After taking on increasing debt to keep the farm going, Frank Jr falls ill. Before he dies, he tells his son Eric that he should not feel obligated to keep photographing the tree. Nevertheless, Eric feels compelled to continue the project.

Years later, in 1979, twenty-five-year-old Nicholas Hoel and his parents are staying with his grandmother for Christmas. Nick loves the photographs of the Hoel Chestnut (now numbering a thousand). An art graduate, he has repeatedly sketched the tree planted by his great-great-great-grandfather.

Nick drives to see an exhibition in Omaha, but the rest of his family elect to stay at the farmhouse. On the way back, driving through snow, he has a near miss with a truck and spends the night in his car at the side of the road. The next morning, returning to the farmhouse, he finds his father's body lying at the foot of the stairs. Upstairs his mother and grandmother are lying in their beds, dead. Nick realizes that his family has been gassed by the propane heater. He staggers outside and falls into the snow underneath the chestnut tree.

Mimi Ma

In Shanghai, 1948, Ma Sih Hsuin prepares to travel from Shanghai to San Francisco where he is to become a graduate student of engineering. He is leaving on the insistence of his father who predicts that the family and their business will be finished once the Communist party establishes itself in China. The Ma family's considerable fortune has been built upon silk plantations.

Before Ma Sih Hsuin leaves, his father gives him valuable family heirlooms to take with him: three jade rings and an ancient scroll. The scroll shows three old men who have reached the final stage of Enlightenment.

In the USA Ma Sih Hsuin goes by the name of Winston Ma. He marries and plants a mulberry tree in his backyard as a reminder of the silk trees that made his family's fortune in China. In 1958 their first child, Mimi, is born. Her arrival is followed by two more daughters: Carmen and Amelia.

During Mimi's childhood her father invents a cell phone while her mother begins to show signs of early onset dementia. Mimi studies literature at college but then transfers to Berkeley to become an engineer, like her father. After graduating, she works as a casting process supervisor for a ceramics business in Portland. Meanwhile, the family mulberry tree succumbs to disease. Winston calls Mimi and sadly tells her that he and his "silk farm" are coming to the end of the road. That fall, Winston sits under the dying mulberry tree and kills himself with a Smith & Wesson. After his death the sisters divide the inherited jade rings between them. Each of the rings is carved with a tree and represents an aspect of time. Mimi chooses the mulberry ring which symbolizes the future. The sisters agree that Mimi should have the scroll appraised.

Adam Appich

Adam is the youngest of four children whose births have all been commemorated by the planting of a tree. Adam's is a maple, his brother Emmett is ironwood and his sisters, Leigh and Jean, are elm and ash. Adam is the least "normal" of the Appich clan and finds social interaction difficult.

When Adam's mother falls pregnant again the family discusses what type of tree should commemorate the new arrival. The decision-making process makes Adam anxious as he believes that their choice will define who the new sibling will become. In the end, his father chooses black walnut because it is on sale. As his father is about to plant the tree, Adam is distressed to see that its roots still have cloth wound around them. He jumps into the hole to stop the "murder" and almost breaks his legs. After the walnut tree is planted, he continues to worry that it will die and his baby brother, Charles, will follow. As it turns out, walnut is an appropriate choice for Charles who grows into a tough, ruthless individual. Both he and the tree thrive.

By the age of ten, Adam has become a loner, more interested in wildlife than humans. When his mother throws his collection of specimens away, dismissing it as "bug-infested junk." Adam slaps her. In return, his father twists and fractures Adam's wrist. When his cast comes off Adam climbs his maple and stays there for a long time.

Dutch elm disease has been making its way across the country for years. When Leigh's elm yellows with the disease, Adam is the only one to notice. After the tree dies, he makes a plaque from the wood engraved with the words, "A tree is a passage between earth and sky." Leigh moves out and leaves the plaque behind.

By 1976 Adam is thirteen and obsessed with ants. Fascinated by their purpose and group organization, he paints them with different hues of nail varnish to keep track of their movements. Concluding that ants silently pass signals to one another, he enters a science fair with his observations. He fails to win a medal as the judges refuse to believe his research is the original work of a child.

That spring Leigh goes on vacation with friends. She is reported missing after getting into a convertible with a stranger and is never seen again. Grief-stricken, Adam's parents argue, and his mother's elbow is broken in one of their fights. As the search for Leigh proves fruitless, Adam's mother becomes addicted to prescription drugs and sinks into depression. Adam becomes increasingly aware of the self-destructive nature of humans and reads *The Ape Inside Us* by R.M. Rabinowski. The book explains that human behaviour is driven by predictable impulses. Adam writes to the author (a professor of psychology) and tells him that the book has changed his life. As Adam had hoped, Rabinowski replies inviting him to apply for a place at Fortuna College.

Ray Brinkman & Dorothy Cazaly

When Ray and Dorothy first meet, he is a junior intellectual property lawyer and she a stenographer. Dorothy agrees to go on a date with Ray on the condition that they audition together for an amateur production of *Macbeth*. She is cast as Lady Macbeth, he as Macduff.

Before they marry, Dorothy breaks off the relationship several times, fearing the commitment and the prospect of being owned. Ray writes a letter to Dorothy suggesting that they should mark every wedding anniversary by planting something in the garden and watching it grow. As Dorothy reads the letter, she drives into a linden tree.

Douglas Pavlicek

In 1971, nineteen-year-old Douglas agrees to take part in the Stanford Prison Experiment conducted by the Psychology Department of Stanford University. He is arrested and taken to a simulated prison where he becomes Prisoner 571. The experiment soon gets out of hand when some of the "prisoners" rise up against "guards" who are abusing their power. The rebellious prisoners are placed in solitary confinement and the guards promise privileges to anyone who will name the ringleaders of the uprising. Douglas refuses to crack, despite the fact that the most basic human necessities have been redefined as "privileges." The guards announce that if one of the prisoners will give up his blanket for the night, a fellow prisoner will be released from solitary confinement. Douglas does not give up his blanket but cannot sleep. After six days the experiment comes to a premature end.

Shortly after his release, Douglas signs up to become a loadmaster in the U.S. Air Force fighting in Vietnam. During one mission his aircraft is hit and catches on fire. Douglas escapes from the plane but his parachute tangles and he accidentally discharges the gun strapped to his thigh. Shot in the leg, he lands in Nakhon Ratchasima Province, Thailand, in the branches of a vast fig tree. Pilgrims arrive to worship at the tree just as Douglas falls from its branches.

Douglas returns to the USA and is awarded a medal for bravery. He sells his medal and spends the next nine years drifting from job to job. One day, after leaving a position at a horse ranch, he drives aimlessly and stops at the side of a road to relieve himself. Stepping into apparently dense woodland, he is shocked to discover that, beyond the trees that line the road, the forest has been cleared. Stopping off at a gas station, he learns from the cashier that National Forests (unlike National Parks) are not protected from development. Douglas is furious, convinced that the "beauty strips" of trees along roadsides are designed to hide what is really going on from the public. He hires a pilot to take him up in a plane to see just how extensively the forest has been cleared. Horrified by what he sees, he takes a job planting Douglas-fir seedlings into cleared land.

Neelay Mehta

Neelay lives with his Indian parents in San Jose, California. When he turns eight his father brings home a computer kit for them to make together. From that moment he is obsessed with the possibilities of computer programming.

When he is eleven, Neelay's literature teacher catches him working on his latest programming idea in class. She confiscates his notebook and he swears at her. On the way home, Neelay dwells on the shame his parents will feel when they discover he is in trouble at school. He climbs an *encina* (oak) tree in the park and considers inflicting a minor injury on himself to distract his parents from his crime. Changing his mind, he decides to go home and face the music but slips on his descent. When he hits the ground, he cracks his spine. The accident leaves Neelay paralyzed from the waist down.

At the age of seventeen Neelay secures a place at Stanford University studying computing. Inspired by some outlandish-looking trees he sees on campus he creates free games situated on other planets.

Patricia Westerford

Growing up in the 1950s, Patricia has both a hearing and speech impediment. Her problems in communicating isolate her from her peers, but she shares a close bond with her father Bill. She inherits his love of botany and they conduct an experiment together, observing a beech tree. When Patricia is fifteen her father dies in a car accident. After his death, she writes up her observations on the beech tree and replants it in a spot where she and her father used to sit together.

Patricia goes to Eastern Kentucky University where her obsession with botany earns her the nickname "Plant-Patty." As a graduate she goes to Forestry school but disagrees with some of the most fundamental premises she is taught there. While her professors claim that forests should be managed by clearing dead trees from the forest floor, she knows that dead trees are vital for the life cycles of insects and birds. She also disagrees with the field's focus on productivity over biodiversity.

During research for her doctorate Patricia discovers evidence that, when infested with parasites, trees alert other trees to the danger by releasing airborne chemicals. This supports her belief that trees not only communicate with each other, but also protect each other. She publishes her theories under the gender-neutral name Dr Pat Westerford.

When Patricia's discoveries are published by a journal, the popular press takes an interest. Patricia is interviewed and more articles are written about her theory that trees communicate with each other. A few months later, three notable male dendrologists publish an open letter mocking Patricia's scientific conclusions and claiming that her methodology was flawed. The letter also draws attention to the fact that Dr Westerford is a woman. Newspapers print articles to say that Patricia's findings have been discredited. Her lectureship contract is not renewed.

With her academic career in tatters, Patricia teaches in high school. Depressed and purposeless, she decides to commit suicide by eating a deadly fungus found during a woodland walk. At the last moment, she changes her mind and vows that she will never again worry about public opinion.

For the next few years Patricia works odd jobs, spending as much time as she can in the woods. In the early 1980s she travels north-west and takes a job with the Bureau of Land Management as a wilderness ranger. Meanwhile, back in civilization, a journal article appears that supports and builds upon Patricia's earlier research.

When Patricia meets two wildlife researchers in the forest, one of them recognizes her name and invites her to join his team. Patricia agrees and is surprised to find that she enjoys working with like-minded colleagues. Researching Douglas-firs, she discovers that the roots of separate trees sometimes conjoin when they meet. Over time, Patricia develops a friendship with the research station manager, Dennis Ward. Eventually they decide to marry but retain separate homes.

Olivia Vandergriff

In 1989 Olivia is in her senior year at university studying actuarial science. Her hedonistic lifestyle, involving partying, sex and drugs, means that she is in danger of failing her course. After announcing to her housemates that her divorce has finally come through, she gets high and takes a shower. Falling into bed, she reaches for the lamp switch with her wet hand. She is electrocuted and dies.

TRUNK

When Olivia's body hits the floor, the force restarts her heart. Her ex-husband discovers her and takes her to the hospital. Before medics can perform a brain scan, Olivia absconds from the hospital and shuts herself in her room for two days. Convinced that higher powers are trying to speak to her, she throws away her drugs and alcohol. She misses her final exams and tells her parents she will not be coming home for Christmas.

When Olivia's housemates return after Christmas, they are wary of her personality change. Once the most hedonistic of the group, Olivia now pities her housemates when they drink and take drugs. One day the higher voices return while Olivia is sitting in a college auditorium. She follows their instructions, leaving the lecture to drive for hours toward the Midwest. After sleeping in her car, she sees "beings of light." Going into a store to use the bathroom, her attention is caught by a news broadcast on the TV. The broadcast shows environmental activists in Solace, California, protesting against the felling of ancient redwood trees. The voices tell her that it is her mission to join the protesters.

Years earlier, Ray and Dorothy return home from performing in an amateur production of *Who's Afraid of Virginia Woolf?* Dorothy is now forty-two and over the past few years they have spent thousands of dollars on unsuccessful fertility treatments. Devastated at the news that they have run out of options she drunkenly tries to pick a fight with her husband. For the past two years they have forgotten to honour their anniversary ritual.

Olivia sees a banner at the side of the road advertising "free tree art" and pulls over. A man greets her, introducing himself as Nick Hoel. He tells her that he has been working on images of the same chestnut tree for the past nine years—artwork based on photographs taken by several generations of his family. Nick explains that the farmhouse he lives in belonged to his family but has now been sold on, and the chestnut tree is dying. Olivia tells him about her life-changing electrocution and the protest she saw on TV. Nick decides that he will accompany Olivia on her journey. Before they leave, they bury his artwork in the ground behind the farmhouse.

After her father's death, Mimi throws herself into work and hobbies. She is promoted and has a series of short relationships with men and women. In remembrance of her father, she displays his scroll on her office wall and wears the jade ring.

From Mimi's office in Portland there is a view of Ponderosa pine in the park below. When two of her colleagues argue over the distinctive scent of Ponderosa pine (vanilla versus turpentine) Mimi

24

goes outside to sniff them. Breathing in their scent, she feels as if her father is present and experiences a moment of enlightenment. From a nearby poster she learns that the city council are proposing to cut down the pines. A public hearing is scheduled at the town hall for those who oppose it. She begins to spend her lunch break sitting under the trees.

In a bar in Oregon, Douglas celebrates the planting of his "fifty thousandth tree." His triumphant mood is shattered when a fellow drinker tells him that timber companies plant saplings as it allows them to increase their felling quotas and cut down more ancient woodland. Douglas faces the fact that he has wasted the last four years of his life and actively contributed to deforestation. Feeling purposeless, he wanders around Portland and sees the sign for the town hall meeting. After locating the condemned Ponderosa pine, he falls asleep underneath them. Just after midnight he is woken by the sound of trucks and chainsaws as workers prepare to cut down the trees. Douglas tries to stop them, telling the men that the public hearing has not yet taken place. The men reply that they are following city orders. Douglas tries to climb one of the trees, but the workers pull him down and hold him until the police arrive. He is charged with "obstructing official business." The following day, Mimi arrives at work and is horrified to see that the trees have gone.

Douglas appears in court, receiving a suspended sentence and three days' labour planting ashes for the city. At the library he researches "guerrilla forestry," learning about a group of protesters who are blockading logging roads. Returning to the location of the felled Ponderosa pine, he uses a magic marker to mark out every quarter-century of rings on their stumps. Around the edge of the stumps he writes "CUT DOWN WHILE YOU SLEPT." Mimi comes out of her office and angrily confronts Douglas, assuming that he is a city employee. When she understands his real aim, she apologizes. Douglas, meanwhile, immediately falls for Mimi.

Ray and Dorothy have given up amateur dramatics and spend a lot of their time reading. Ray favours non-fiction, while Dorothy reads fiction. Ray suggests that they convert the room previously reserved for a baby into built-in bookshelves. Their anniversary arrives and, again, they forget to mark it with a plant. Dorothy becomes addicted to sexual encounters with strangers. Ray knows that Dorothy is being unfaithful but says nothing.

25

Nick and Olivia arrive in Solace, California, and are overwhelmed by the size and majesty of the redwoods. They join the camp of activists who call themselves the Life Defense Force. Mother N, the spokesperson of the group, is committed to non-violent protest. She explains that Humboldt Timber is felling old-growth trees as quickly as possible before legislation is brought in to stop it. Many of the trees are hundreds of years old. Nick paints the faces of the activists, transforming them into woodland creatures. Each of the group takes on a new name. Nick becomes Watchman while Olivia takes the name Maidenhair.

In Redwood City, California, Neelay launches his first profitable game. When it sells out, he expands his business and names it Sempervirens. On the verge of accepting a takeover bid for the company, he visits the exotic trees on the Stanford campus hoping for a sign that he is doing the right thing. The trees prove unresponsive, but he remembers seeing a huge redwood tree with his father when he was a child. Realizing that this redwood subconsciously inspired his company name, he decides he must consult the tree.

Driving to the redwood in the middle of the night, Neelay is overcome by its vastness and decides that he cannot sell his company. He begins working on a new game where players emerge in an uninhabited and unspoiled area of Earth. As players develop their land by farming, building and cutting down trees, other players will be doing the same within their own allocated area. In time, players will try to take over the land of others. Neelay calls the game *Mastery* and it proves to be hugely addictive and successful. Neelay barely sleeps or eats, consumed by ideas to develop it even further. His success allows him to buy his parents a luxury home, but he leads a lonely life. Self-conscious about his appearance, he is a virtual recluse, avoiding human contact as much as possible.

Olivia and Nick take part in a roadblock of Highway 36. Dressed as a big cat, Olivia crosses a traverse line between two trees to unfurl a banner. On Olivia's whistle, her fellow activists, also dressed as animals, emerge from coffins. The protest makes the news.

In a lecture hall at Fortuna College, Adam listens to Professor Rabinowski's lecture on the power of social programming. Partway through, the professor looks uncomfortable and excuses himself.

Remaining seated in the auditorium, the students hear a commotion in the hallway. Like the rest of the audience, Adam does not move and whispers to a female student that the professor is demonstrating "the bystander effect." Out in the hallway Professor Rabinowski dies of a heart attack.

Adam goes to Santa Cruz to begin research for a doctorate. He quickly earns the nickname "Bias Boy" due to his conviction that social conformity prevents humans from acting independently. For his thesis, he decides to investigate the personality traits that allow some people to see beyond group mentality. His thesis advisor suggests he should study activists who are fighting for the rights of trees.

Mimi and Douglas join activists on a Forest Service road in the Western Cascades. The protest is a peaceful one, coming to an end when police officers arrive and handcuff the activists. Mimi tells one of the officers she needs to urinate, but he ignores her, and eventually she is forced to wet herself where she stands. She and Douglas are arrested and booked at the police station.

Patricia writes *The Secret Forest*—a book about how trees communicate, cooperate and look after each other. After it is published, she receives a large sum of money from her agent demonstrating just how well it is selling. She also receives letters from readers describing how the book has changed their perception of trees.

Olivia volunteers to tree-sit an old-growth redwood to prevent it from being felled. She and Nick are now a couple and he accompanies her. The enormous tree is known as Mimas and they set up camp on a platform two hundred feet from the ground. Their bedroom is a tarp shelter and their bathroom is a bucket. Olivia reads *The Secret Forest*, aloud. After two weeks in Mimas, the nights become colder and Olivia and Nick battle frostbite. One night, strong winds nearly blow them off the platform. Teams of loggers and representatives from the logging company fail to persuade them to come down.

Mimi pays a fine of $300 for "unlawful assembly" and continues to join protests with Douglas. Arriving at one peaceful protest, they see loggers drive a loader while two women are still chained to it. Some of the protesters, including Douglas, climb nearby trees and the loggers begin felling dangerously close to them. The police arrive in riot gear and begin to handcuff the protesters. Only

Douglas remains in the treetops, having handcuffed himself to the trunk. Climbing ladders to reach Douglas, police officers cut away his jeans and blast his exposed groin with pepper spray. Continuing the assault, they order him to unlock himself. Finally, Douglas manages to whisper that he has dropped the key and the police cut him down. After being processed at the police station, Mimi takes Douglas home. She wants to tend to his injuries, but Douglas is too ashamed to let her see his bright orange genitalia.

Neelay continues to release new improved versions of *Mastery*, obsessed with creating detailed biodiversity in his virtual world. Living in an apartment above his company's headquarters, he becomes increasingly frail and rarely leaves his chair, even to sleep. Whenever his mother calls, she expresses concern that he does not have a life partner. In the end, Neelay lies, telling his mother that he is in a relationship with one of his caregivers. Slamming his hand down onto his desk in frustration, he feels his bones break.

Patricia appears in court as an expert educating witness, hoping to convince the judge to place an injunction on logging in "sensitive" federal areas. Terrified of speaking in public, her old speech defect makes a reappearance. Arguing the importance of preserving the 2–3% of old-growth forest that remains, however, she becomes increasingly eloquent. The judge reveals that he has read Patricia's book and places an injunction on new sales of public forest in Western Oregon. After Patricia's victory, the opposing expert witness predicts that, in the light of the ruling, timber companies with existing rights on private land will fell their trees as quickly as possible.

Mimi and Douglas join a protest at the offices of a tree milling business where the activists chain themselves to a pillar in the reception area. When the police arrive, the protesters are warned that pepper spray will be used if they refuse to leave. The officers apply a solution of concentrated pepper to the protesters' eyes with Q-tips. Although screaming with pain, the activists refuse to release themselves. When Mimi receives this treatment, Douglas launches himself at the officers. He is handcuffed and arrested.

Patricia learns that the court injunction is not going to be enforced. She decides that, as half the world's tree species have already been destroyed, she will start a seed bank to try to save the rest.

Dorothy tells Ray that their marriage is over. In turmoil, he watches news coverage of environmental activists being peppered in the eyes. He has a stroke and collapses. Later, in hospital, he undergoes surgery but is left paralyzed and unable to speak.

Mimi arrives at work to find that she has been fired as a result of her criminal activities appearing all over the news. She is escorted off the premises. Meanwhile, Douglas is punched in the face by a "friend" who has tired of hearing his views on deforestation. He decides to drive to Mimi's condo and fails to notice that a logging truck is following him. The truck rams Douglas's rear bumper, spinning him around and leaving him in the intersection of the highway. Shaken, he arrives at Mimi's condo where a drunken Mimi pulls him inside.

Adam climbs Mimas to interview Olivia and Nick for his doctoral research on environmental activists. When he asks them to fill out a questionnaire, Olivia suggests that he will learn more by just talking to them. During their conversation Adam begins to argue that, if there were a genuine environmental crisis, more people would be taking action. As he does so, he realizes that he is describing the bystander effect.

A Life Defense Force member breaks the news that two of their group—Mother N and Moses— have been killed by a bomb. The police claim that Mother N and Moses accidentally blew themselves up with explosives obtained for eco-terrorism. Nick and Olivia are certain that this version of events cannot be true, as Mother N was opposed to violence of any kind. Adam chooses to spend the night in Mimas with Olivia and Nick. The next morning a helicopter flies dangerously close to them and bulldozers begin to ram the tree's trunk. Unable to hold on any longer, Olivia and Nick agree to come down. All three are taken into custody.

Meanwhile, Mimi and Douglas protest at Deep Creek woods where 10,000 acres have been destroyed by an unidentified arsonist. The fire has conveniently allowed the Forest Service to cut and sell the lightly damaged standing trees.

After several days in custody, Adam, Nick and Olivia are released without charge. They go back to the site of their protest to find that Mimas and all the trees surrounding him have been felled. Olivia and Nick plan to travel to Oregon to join another resistance group and invite Adam to join them. Adam turns the invitation down, choosing to return to Santa Cruz to write up his findings. One evening, he emerges from the student bar and is hit on the head by a falling piece of eucalyptus bark. Turning to the eucalyptus tree, he asks it what it wants.

Having almost completed his thesis, Adam travels to Olivia's new protest site. When he arrives at the encampment on a Forest Service road, he meets Douglas and Mimi who introduce themselves as Doug-fir and Mulberry. Thinking of his birth tree, Adam introduces himself as Maple. News reaches the group that the American president is taking their protest seriously and is considering a review of policy. Shortly afterwards, a convoy of vehicles arrives at the camp and the protesters are given ten minutes to leave. When they resist, an excavator begins to batter the wall the activists have built as a fortification. Mimi climbs a tree, but when an excavator shakes it, she falls and impales her cheek on a broken pole. Douglas runs to her but is caught by the claw of the excavator as it swings back. Mimi is left with horrific facial injuries, while Douglas lies unconscious. At the hospital, Douglas has surgery on his fractured leg while Mimi has her cheek roughly patched back into place. The police do not charge them.

Olivia, Nick, Mimi, Douglas, and Adam begin a series of raids destroying timber industry property with explosives. Their final target is the construction office on a public forest site recently sold off to private developers. As the others plant explosives around the building, Nick graffities nearby trailers. When the devices are detonated the explosion is far larger than intended. Caught in the blast, Olivia lies on the ground, fatally injured. Mimi tells Adam to drive to the nearest town and get the police. Adam hesitates, certain that Olivia is beyond medical help and fearful of being arrested. In her last moments of life, Olivia tells them to finish the job. She dies and a distraught Nick blames Adam for failing to fetch help.

CROWN

After placing Olivia's dead body in the flames of the explosion, Douglas, Mimi and Adam force Nick into the van. When they reach Portland, they go their separate ways. They all agree to say nothing and protect each other.

Consumed by loss, Nick moves into a rundown cabin close to Mimas's stump, hoping for some kind of message from Olivia. Adam returns to Santa Cruz to submit his thesis, and Mimi sells her condo. When Olivia's bones are discovered at the site of the explosion, news stories focus on the graffiti found nearby and suggest that it is the work of a serial killer.

After a heavy downpour, Nick sees the beginnings of a landslide on the nearby mountain. He escapes his cabin just before it is swept away and alerts his neighbours, leading them to safety. The landslide is brought to a halt by a barrier of redwood trees that remain standing. Nick looks back at the life-saving redwoods and sees that their trunks are painted with blue X's—a sign that they will be felled the following week.

Mimi has her father's scroll appraised by an art dealer. He offers her a sum large enough to ensure that she, her sisters, and their children will be comfortable for the rest of their lives. She agrees to the sale, believing this is what her father would have wanted.

Dorothy has stayed with Ray who remains largely paralyzed and can only communicate through mostly indecipherable sounds. In the day, she looks after him and reads to him and every evening she goes out to meet Alan—the man she would marry if she were not still married to Ray. One day Ray signals that he wants Dorothy to read out the crossword clues— a ritual from before he had his stroke. Dorothy reads out the clues to humour him. Hours later, Ray gestures for a pen and scribbles "Releaf"—the correct answer to one of the crossword clues.

Neelay plays *Mastery* incognito to gain feedback on the game. He meets another player who complains that the game has come to reflect the real world, with players obsessing over acquiring more and more commodities.

Nick travels around the country working various jobs. At night he walks through the neighbourhoods of the city graffitiing walls.

Adam becomes an associate professor and lives in Columbus, Ohio. Watching the news, he sees that the recent bombing of a research laboratory has been linked to similar attacks over the last few years. He immediately recognizes the words that have been graffitied on a wall at the research lab —"CONTROL KILLS/CONNECTION HEALS."

In San Francisco Mimi is working on a master's degree when she reads about an explosion in a lumberyard. Like Adam, she recognizes the slogans that were painted at the scene. The news report states that the police are investigating connections with eco-terrorist acts committed between 1980 and 1999. Mimi believes that it is only a matter of time before they are all arrested.

As the end of 1999 approaches, Douglas is living in Montana as the out-of-season caretaker of a deserted mining town. He is also working on a "Manifesto of Failure"—a private memoir of his time as an activist. One day he walks along a snowy mountain ridge which gives way beneath him. Falling 200 feet, he is saved when he manages to hold onto a tree trunk. Tempted to give up and just lay in the snow, Douglas revives when he sees Olivia kneeling beside him. She tells him that he has not yet done everything he needs to do.

Now in her sixties, Patricia travels the world collecting seeds and giving speeches. During her globe-trotting she witnesses different versions of old-growth deforestation—rainforests replaced by oil palm plantations, ancient Japanese forests replaced by pines, Thai teak replaced by eucalyptus. In the Amazon rainforest she is shown a tree which looks astonishingly like a woman. When she returns home, Patricia shows a photograph of the "tree woman" to Dennis. He suggests that she could use the image in support of her work. That night, Dennis dies in his sleep.

In 2001 Dorothy's relationship with Alan comes to an end when she makes it clear that she will not leave Ray. One day she is alarmed to hear Ray cry out with distress. She goes into his room to see the second of the Twin Towers disintegrating on live news.

Having changed her name to Judith Hanson, Mimi now works as a therapist. During her unconventional therapy sessions, she holds a client's gaze for several hours, conducting a dialogue with them without speaking.

Arriving back in Iowa, Nick drives to his family's old farmhouse to find it is now a factory. The Hoel Chestnut has been cut down. When night falls, he digs up his artwork and the photographs of the tree. As he takes them to his car, the police arrive. The police officers let him go after determining that the property's new owner is not interested in prosecuting him.

After reading *The Secret Forest*, Neelay tries to explain to his team why he feels that *Mastery* has lost its way. He suggests that, instead of offering players limitless resources, the point of the game should be to learn how to balance the world's existing resources. Uneasy at the prospect of sacrificing the game's huge profitability, Neelay's team votes overwhelmingly against him.

Douglas tells a young Eastern European woman how he

dragged himself back to town and was helicoptered to hospital after falling from the mountainside. When the woman tells Douglas that she has nowhere to stay, he invites her back to his cabin. Douglas is attracted to his guest but, when she kisses him, he cries and tells her that he does not love her. He gives the woman his bed for the night and guesses, from the light that remains on in the room, that she stays up late reading. She leaves the next morning. Two months later, federal officers arrest Douglas and search his cabin. When they take away his journal Douglas realizes that his Eastern European guest must have read it.

In 2011 Adam walks through the Occupy Wall Street protest in Zuccotti Park. He browses through the People's Library and comes across a copy of his childhood favourite—*The Golden Guide to Insects*. Inside someone has written the name "Raymond B." Shortly afterwards Adam is surprised to bump into Douglas. Adam tells Douglas that he is now married, has a five-year-old son and is a professor of psychology at NYU. Douglas says he is between jobs and visiting a friend. The two men talk about their time as activists, the arson they committed and Olivia's death. Before they part, Douglas asks Adam why he failed to go for help when Olivia was dying. Adam justifies his actions, saying that Olivia would still have died, and they would all have gone to prison.

Adam is giving a lecture to his students when three armed FBI officers arrive. When the lecture ends the officers lead him away in handcuffs. Adam realizes that his meeting with Douglas was not coincidental and that Douglas recorded the conversation.

Dorothy takes a copy of *The Secret Forest* out of the library and reads it aloud to Ray. The book changes their perception of the trees in their garden. The couple embarks on a project to identify and learn about them all. One of the largest trees turns out to be one of the few mature American chestnuts left in the country. Ray says that he planted the chestnut with their daughter.

The FBI cuts Douglas a deal in exchange for the information he gave about Adam. Instead of life imprisonment for domestic terrorism he receives a seven-year sentence in a medium-security prison with eligibility for early parole. When first interviewed, he unsuccessfully tried to persuade FBI agents that his journal was a novel. Confronted with photographs of activists, however, he was pressurized to reveal the real name of at least one of his conspirators. He chose to identify Adam as Maple, largely to protect Mimi's identity.

After finishing her latest book, Patricia travels to an environmental conference in California. She delivers a speech comparing man's destruction of the environment to "suicide" and shows the audience a glass vial containing plant extracts. In answer to the central question of the conference—what is the most effective thing a person can do for the planet's future? — she pours the contents of the vial into her drinking water.

For four years, Adam has lived with his family under the conditions of house arrest. Fitted with a tracker around his ankle, he is not allowed to leave the building without permission. Outside his window he sees colourful paint bombs being dropped from passing cars, creating the effect of a giant tree. Realizing that the demonstration is for him, he leaves the building without asking for clearance. When his anklet alarm goes off, he quickly returns to his apartment.

Mimi is attending the environmental conference, listening to Patricia's speech. When the botanist lifts her glass, apparently about to drink, Mimi catches her eye, holding her gaze. Mentally she pleads with Patricia not to commit suicide. In response, Patricia silently argues that the gesture will momentarily catch the world's attention. Also in the audience is Neelay. While everyone else sits paralyzed, he waves his arms and shouts, trying to stand. The future diverges into two possibilities—Patricia drinks the solution, or she declares a toast to "unsuicide" and throws it toward the audience.

Adam's wife tries to persuade him to give the FBI information on his fellow activists. She points out that the alternative is to go to prison for life and allow his son to grow up without a father. When the court case finally dawns, Adam refuses to incriminate anyone else. He is found guilty of domestic terrorism and given a sentence of 140 years.

Ray and Dorothy decide to stop mowing the garden and leave it to grow. The small patch of wilderness will be their legacy for the next generation. Dorothy ignores complaints from the neighbours and warnings from the city that she will be fined. When a team of young men arrive, sent by the city to tidy up the garden, she sends them away. If necessary, she is prepared to lose everything she has in the legal battle that is sure to follow.

SEEDS

In San Francisco, Mimi hears about Adam's sentencing on the news and realizes that Douglas must have betrayed him. Understanding that his motive must have been to protect her, she feels guilty for retaining her freedom. She also knows that if she gives herself up, Douglas's sacrifice will be rendered pointless.

In prison, Douglas listens to an audio course on dendrology narrated by Patricia Westerford. He has discovered a hard lump in his side but decides not to get it checked out.

Neelay hires coders to help him with his ambitious new project. His work leads to the creation of digital entities called "Learners" who gather and analyze information on the natural world. Their aim is to work out if and how people can live in harmony with other living creatures. Over time, the learners evolve, merging together and creating a "living code." In the future this new digital species will be able to translate the language of trees so that humans can understand them. Neelay knows that he will not live long enough to see his work's fruition but is satisfied that he has helped to develop it.

Adam is taken to prison where he will be assaulted many times by fellow inmates. As he is checked in, he notices that a sticky burr has miraculously attached itself to his sleeve during the journey.

When Ray hears of Adam's sentencing on the news, he suggests that Adam's legal team could have argued "Self-defense." Ray dies before Dorothy has the chance to read him *The New Metamorphosis* by Patricia Westerford.

Sitting under a pine tree Mimi takes off her jade ring and leaves it in the grass. She experiences a moment of enlightenment where she hears the truths communicated by the trees. They tell her that the Earth will be transformed by a series of natural disasters. Only after that will people relearn how to live in harmony with nature.

Nick continues to create eco-art wherever he travels. As he works on a huge design made from rotted tree trunks in the woods, a Native American joins him. Soon others join them to help. When the project is completed the logs spell "STILL." The word will be seen by satellites in orbit for the next two hundred years until it disappears back into the forest floor.

STYLE

An Epic

In more than one review, *The Overstory* has been compared to *Moby Dick*. Herman Melville's story of man versus whale has become the benchmark against which many hefty tomes with big themes are compared. In the case of *The Overstory*, there is some justification for the comparison. At 500 pages, it is round about the same length. Like Melville's novel, it is also concerned with man's compulsion to dominate the natural world. If anything, however, *The Overstory* is more epic in its scope, hugely ambitious in the ground it covers.

The plot of *The Overstory* largely focuses on North American deforestation during the late twentieth and early twenty-first centuries. With extraordinary skill, however, Powers also places his story within the context of American history as a whole. Beginning with a mid-nineteenth-century pioneer and the chestnut trees he plants in Iowa, the author traces the history of American trees alongside the history of humans. During the years when his characters suffer the effects of two world wars, we are reminded that another mass loss of life took place—the decimation of the American chestnut population by blight spread from an imported tree. In this way, the lives of trees and humans are seamlessly intertwined.

An Eco-Novel

The Overstory is a big book tackling big themes. There are few topics more pressing than impending ecological catastrophe and Powers is not afraid to address it. In doing so, he makes a brave choice, for eco-fiction is not the easiest genre to write. While there have been many critically acclaimed novels dramatizing the potential consequences of ecological disaster (e.g. Margaret Atwood's *Oryx and Crake*, or Cormac McCarthy's *The Road*) there are fewer that depict the slow decline towards the point of no return. One of the challenges facing authors is the difficulty of creating drama out of something which—despite all the evidence—we still do not seem to consider a crisis. If people are apathetic about climate change, then why would they read a novel about it? There is also the thorny issue that, generally, fiction readers do not like to be preached at. Successfully negotiating these factors takes a skilled writer indeed.

Structure

One of the most technically impressive elements of *The Overstory* is the way in which its structure echoes its subject matter. Split into sections titled "Roots", "Trunk", "Crown" and "Seeds", the narrative is shaped like a tree.

In "Roots", which takes up the first third of the novel, nine main characters are introduced in what appears to be a succession of short stories. While these stories seem unrelated to each other, the life of each character is interwoven in some way with the lives of trees.

In "Trunk," the disparate characters begin to join like roots at the base of the tree trunk. Five of the characters (Olivia, Nick, Mimi, Douglas and Adam) actually meet, joining forces to protest against the logging of old-growth trees. Independently, Patricia is working on scientific work with a very similar aim. Meanwhile, subtle links between these stories and those of Neelay and the Brinkmans are established.

In "Crown" (which, for non-tree buffs, describes the leaves and branches at the top of the tree), the characters' actions come to a head. Ray has a stroke and Olivia dies, splitting the group and sending them down different pathways, like tree branches. "Seeds" then looks at the immediate and long-term consequences of the characters' actions. This means not only their individual fates (prison, possible suicide, etc.) but the legacies they will leave behind (Patricia's books and seed bank, Neelay's "learners", the Brinkmans' wild garden, and Nick's giant tree sculpture). The novel ends with the possibility that these legacies, along with Adam's sacrifice, may combine to effect a change in public consciousness.

Character Connections

Even before some of the main characters meet, we are told that "their lives have long been connected, deep underground." This idea of hidden connections or roots is a thread that runs through the whole of *The Overstory*. Some of the characters are literally drawn together by their common fight against deforestation. Others never meet, but subtle connections between them emerge "like an unfolding book." An entire guide could be devoted to these connections, but the following are some of the most notable.

— Patricia does not meet the other main characters but most of them read, and are deeply influenced by her book, *The Secret Forest*.

— Neelay and Mimi separately attend the conference where Patricia gives a speech on the best way to save the planet. Both try to intervene when it seems she is about to commit public suicide.

— In prison, Douglas listens to an audio course on dendrology in his cell, narrated by Patricia.

— As children, Adam and Patricia both experience communication problems and find human interaction challenging. Both are more interested in wildlife than humans.

— Adam's childhood observations of ant communication systems echo the research undertaken by Patricia on tree communication. Like Patricia, Adam suffers the humiliation of having his work dismissed when the judges of a science fair conclude that it cannot be the work of a child.

— The Brinkmans' favourite tree, like the Hoel Chestnut, is one of the last remaining mature American chestnuts in the country.

— Olivia's father is an intellectual property lawyer like Ray and there are hints that she may be the Brinkmans' daughter.

— Adam comes across a copy of his favourite book as a child (*The Golden Guide to Insects*). The inscription on the title page shows that it once belonged to Ray.

— Ray sees an image on TV of Mimi being peppered in the eyes just before he has a stroke.

— Adam, Winston Ma, Douglas, and Patricia all express the belief that the natural world will return to its rightful order once man has extinguished himself from the planet.

Connections through Language

At several points in the novel, Powers depicts, in rich detail, the complex systems of interdependence that exist within a forest. The complex connections between the people, trees and events in his novel build on these descriptions, turning the narrative into one huge ecosystem where everything is linked. Powers carefully chooses language which magnifies this effect, using words associated with trees and growth in surprising contexts. When, for example, seven-year-old Neelay first begins thinking about the potential of computer programming, his "brain fires and re-wires, building arborized axons, *dendrites*, those tiny spreading trees." Later, he is to discover that "There is a thing in programming called *branching*." Pulling together the associations between two apparently opposing elements (the digital world versus the natural), he reminds us that all things are connected, even if the links are not visible.

Powers also has certain phrases echo and reverberate through the novel. *"Look the color,"* for example, is the phrase that Mimi's father uses when he first shows her the family's ancient Chinese scroll. Later in the novel, these words are repeated as an expression of awe at the beauty of the natural world. Another of Winston's favourite phrases— "What they do?" becomes a blanket expression of disbelief at man's blindness to the destruction he causes. Meanwhile, the Chinese saying quoted by Winston's wife becomes one of the key messages of the novel — "When is the best time to plant a tree? Twenty years ago …When is the next best time? Now."

Narrative Voice

Powers uses multiple intertwined narratives to convey the different viewpoints of his nine protagonists. In the first section of the novel, these individual stories are quite different in pace and tone. Nick's story, for example, has the feel of an epic multigenerational saga. By contrast, the Brinkmans' narrative is a close psychological study of the breakdown of a relationship.

As the individual stories begin to merge, Powers makes use of a more detached, third-person authorial voice. We see this voice used in the italicized passages beginning each section of the novel. Here, unnamed characters are described from a distant, almost godlike, perspective. "Roots" begins with a woman (who we later identify as Mimi) sitting with her back against a tree, listening to what the trees are saying. "Trunk" begins with a man who has ended up in a medium-security prison because of trees—a man who we later realize is Douglas. These passages have the effect of widening the novel's lens for a moment and viewing the characters as part of a larger landscape—one small organism within a vast ecology—before zooming back in again.

Powers also uses this omniscient narrative voice to foreshadow events to come. In "Roots," for example, we learn that Mimi will one day be wanted for arson by the FBI. We are also warned of Ray's impending stroke some time before it happens. This technique echoes the effect of Greek tragedy where the audience knows what is coming, but do not necessarily know how. Suddenly viewed from the perspective of an all-seeing eye, the characters become less individualistic and more allegorical, significant for the small part they play in life's huge pattern.

CHARACTERS

Nicholas Hoel

Nicholas Hoel is the first of the main characters to be introduced in the novel. A Midwesterner who comes from pioneering stock, he has trees in his blood. The original impulse that prompts his Norwegian great-great-great-grandfather to plant chestnuts on his farm in Iowa (over a thousand miles away from their native range) is passed on to successive generations, who embark on a photographic project to capture the tree's essence. Inheriting these photographs, Nick feels that the history of the family is "encoded" in the Hoel Chestnut. As an artist, he is compelled to repeatedly draw and paint it.

Nick's fate echoes that of the Hoel Chestnut. One of six originally planted by Jørgen Hoel, it is the only tree to make it to maturity and, later, becomes one of the few surviving chestnuts in the country after a devastating blight. Nick, too, becomes a sole survivor when the rest of his family is wiped out by a propane heater.

From the age of twenty-five to thirty-five, Nick exists in a kind of limbo, living off his family's life insurance policies. Remaining in the farmhouse, he creates tree art that he cannot sell. All this changes when he meets Olivia. Their meeting comes at a crucial turning point in Nick's life—just as the farmhouse has been sold off and the great chestnut tree has finally succumbed to blight.

Falling in love with Olivia and her sense of purpose, Nick becomes her faithful disciple, following wherever she leads. His quiet yet unshakeable loyalty to her earns him the name Watchman. In the context of the new life she opens up to him, Nick sees the decade he spent creating tree art as preparation for his time as an environmental activist. He utilizes his skills by transforming the faces of fellow activists into those of wild creatures and creating protest graffiti.

41

The time Nick spends with Olivia squatting in the giant redwood, Mimas, is the happiest of his life. After she dies, he is bereft and purposeless, hoping for some sort of sign from beyond the grave. This sign arrives when he and his neighbours survive a mountain landslide thanks to a line of redwood trees scheduled to be felled.

Renewed in his purpose, Nick lives an itinerant life travelling around the country. From the news reports seen by the other characters describing explosions in lumber yards and research laboratories, it is suggested that he continues to engage in extreme activism. He also continues to create eco-art and graffiti, expressing his belief that man needs to heal his damaged relationship with nature. At the end of the novel he completes a huge design from rotted tree trunks, spelling out the word "STILL."

Mimi Ma

The second story to be introduced in the novel is that of Mimi Ma. Mimi is the eldest daughter of Winston Ma, a Chinese engineer who moved to the USA as a young man to escape the communist regime. As a child, she feels little connection to her Chinese heritage, having never met her father's parents. When her father shows her his valuable family heirlooms—jade rings carved with trees and an ancient scroll depicting moments of Enlightenment— they seem nothing more than exotic curios. She also fails to appreciate the significance of the mulberry tree her father plants as a reminder of the silk plantations his family made their fortune from. Her lack of reverence for the tree is demonstrated when she is nine years old and rips off a mulberry leaf "knowing the horror that will follow. Thick, milky tree blood oozes from the wound."

When Mimi's beloved father blows his brains out under the dying mulberry tree, Mimi's feelings turn from apathy to hatred. Linking Winston's suicide to his sad declaration that his silk farm is finished, Mimi blames the tree. Seeing other mulberry's blossoming the following spring, she feels furious at nature's indifference to her personal tragedy.

After her father's death, Mimi throws herself into various hobbies and her engineering career, but her life lacks meaning. Her relationships with men and women remain short-term as she is unwilling to commit to anything more. In memory of her father, she displays the Chinese scroll in her office and wears the jade ring but gives little thought to their deeper significance.

Mimi's moment of epiphany comes when she sniffs the bark of a Ponderosa pine growing in a park outside her office. The scent invokes a strong sense of her father's presence and infuses her with something of his spirit. She begins to share Winston's sense of wonder and respect for the natural world—the feeling that is illustrated on the Chinese scroll depicting three men experiencing the joy of enlightenment. By sniffing the "two-hundred-million-year-old-scent" she forms a connection with her lost father, her Chinese ancestry, and with the universe as a whole.

Mimi's spiritual enlightenment is accompanied by a call to arms—a poster warning that the fragrant pines are scheduled to be cut down by the city. When the trees are felled without the promised public hearing, her anger prompts her to join forces with an unlikely ally in the form of a Vietnam veteran/drifter. Douglas persuades Mimi to join him in a series of environmental protests. Mimi's transformation from pragmatic career woman to eco-activist challenges preconceptions of the typical "tree hugger." In a complete U-turn, she casts off her previous success-oriented goals, her identity as an engineer, and her conformist upbringing.

During her time as an activist Mimi demonstrates absolute commitment to the cause, enduring police brutality, sacrificing her career and eventually suffering a disfiguring facial injury. In the wake of Olivia's death, however, she draws a line under the experience wanting to avoid prison at all costs. Although she cares for Douglas, she is less sentimental about their relationship and makes it clear that they cannot continue to see each other. Selling her father's scroll for an astronomical sum, she begins a new life as Judith Hanson. Under her new identity she develops an unconventional therapy that involves staring into a client's eyes, reading their thoughts, and speaking to them with her mind. This silent form of communication is a gift she has developed through listening to and communing with the natural world.

When Mimi hears about the imprisonment of Douglas and Adam, she feels guilty that she remains free, knowing that Douglas betrayed Adam to save her. She is also aware that, if she gave herself up, the sacrifice of both men would be pointless.

The narrative leaves Mimi as she sits under a pine tree listening to what the trees have to say. They tell her that the Earth will be transformed by a series of natural disasters. Only after that will man learn to live in harmony with his environment.

Adam Appich

From the moment of his birth in 1963, Adam's identity is linked to a tree. The arrival of each of the four Appich siblings is marked by their father planting a tree, and Adam's is a maple. A loner with possible autistic tendencies, Adam finds human behaviour baffling. As a child, however, he is sensitive to the miraculous nature of trees—illustrated when he engraves "A tree is a passage between earth and sky" on a piece of tree bark. Of all the family, he is the only one who takes the tree planting venture seriously. Agonizing over the choice of tree for his new brother (believing that their selection will shape his identity) he is perturbed when his father eventually chooses black walnut for the pragmatic reason that it is on sale. Later, he becomes hysterical when his father plants the walnut tree with clothbound roots, certain that it will signal his brother's demise. As it turns out, Charles and the tree are fine. Later, however, Adam's vision of the world seems to be confirmed when his sister Leigh is abducted and presumed to be dead shortly after her tree succumbs to Dutch elm disease.

Adam's interest in trees extends to wildlife in general. As a teenager, he studies ants, tracking their movements by painting them in different shades of nail varnish. Concluding that ants silently pass signals to one another, he enters a science fair with his observations. He suffers disappointment and humiliation, however, when he fails to win a medal as the judges refuse to believe his research is the work of a child.

Adam's intellectual curiosity turns to psychology when he reads *The Ape Inside Us* by R.M. Rabinowski. Having puzzled over the illogical nature of human behaviour for so long, he believes the book offers the key to understanding it. The promise of discovering scientific patterns within an area previously shrouded in mystery proves irresistible to him. His chosen field of study also teaches Adam how to conform (at least on the surface) with the social expectations of other people.

As a psychology student, Adam concludes that he and his siblings grew up to embody their trees because they were psychologically conditioned to do so. This reflects his growing fascination with "the bystander effect" (the way social conformity prevents people from trying to avert disaster). Despite Adam's academic interest in the bystander effect, he shows that he is not immune to it himself when his mentor, Professor Rabinowski, abruptly excuses himself from the lecture he is giving. Along with the other students, Adam remains seated as he hears a commotion in the hallway (the sound of the professor collapsing and dying of a heart attack). Adam defends his reaction, saying that he believed Rabinowski was demonstrating the bystander effect in action. This intellectual defence does not change the fact that he failed to go to his mentor's assistance.

As a graduate student, Adam decides to interview environmental activists to analyze their personality traits. Having all but forgotten his own childhood connection with trees, he expects to be irritated by the zealotry of the activists. Forced to climb the giant redwood, Mimas, to talk to Olivia and Nick, he wishes he could be safely on the ground analyzing data. His determination to apply strictly scientific methods is then confounded by Olivia's insistence that he will learn more from talking to them than from asking them to fill in a questionnaire.

Adam's first encounter with Olivia proves to be life changing. Like most of the characters who meet her, he falls slightly in love with her. More importantly, he is convinced by her intellectual argument which leads him to question his own beliefs about the future of the planet. Having previously assumed that if the planet were in real danger, people would be making more fuss about it, he realizes that he has been guilty of succumbing to the bystander effect. During this epiphany, the detached scientist in Adam is stripped away as he reconnects with his childhood self—the boy who loved wildlife and preferred to view the world from the top of a maple.

Adam elects to spend the night in Mimas with Olivia and Nick and is present the next day when the protesters are finally forced to descend. Olivia invites him to join them in the next protest but at this point Adam is not quite ready to answer the call. He returns to graduate school but finds that his perspective on life has changed. Shortly afterwards, he joins Olivia and Nick at a protest site where he also meets Mimi and Douglas. From this point, he participates in increasingly extreme protests. After Olivia dies in an explosion, however, he begins to question the wisdom of their actions. He also takes the decision not to fetch the police as Olivia is dying, reasoning that she cannot be saved, and they would all go to prison.

After the activist group disband, Adam retreats into academia. Becoming a respected specialist in his field, he also marries and has a son. His comfortable life is shattered, however, when he is arrested after Douglas betrays him to the FBI. Although his wife begs him to help his case by betraying other members of the group, Adam refuses to do so and receives two consecutive prison sentences of 70 years. Resigned to his fate, he rationalizes that 140 years is nothing in the life of a tree.

Although Adam's commitment to saving trees ebbs and flows in the course of the novel, his final actions demonstrate a final and absolute loyalty to the cause. Like Olivia, he becomes a tree martyr. As he enters the prison where he will spend the rest of his days, readers are informed that he will be assaulted many times by inmates who do not share his beliefs. Still, Adam sees hope in the sticky burr that miraculously attaches itself to his sleeve during his journey from the courthouse to prison.

Ray & Dorothy Brinkman

The story of Dorothy and Ray describes the evolution of a marriage. When the stenographer and intellectual property lawyer meet, it is a case of opposites attracting. While Ray is earnest and responsible, Dorothy is restless and craves excitement. In the early days of their relationship, Dorothy breaks it off with Ray several times, fearing commitment and the prospect of being owned. Once they are married, her continued craving for freedom (as well as their inability to have children) leads her into a succession of self-destructive and indiscreet one-night stands. Patiently, Ray tries to ride the storm until Dorothy announces that their marriage is over.

The massive stroke Ray suffers, leaving him largely paralyzed and brain-damaged, marks a new era in their relationship. Dorothy initially stays and cares for Ray out of guilt, feeling she has been delivered a prison sentence. In the evenings she visits her lover— the man she would marry if Ray had not fallen ill. Slowly, however, Powers illustrates how Dorothy's sense of duty transforms into a genuine commitment to Ray. Going beyond the bounds of taking care of his basic needs, Dorothy reads and chats to her husband, despite little evidence that he hears or understands her. In doing so, she shows a capacity for patience and kindness rarely revealed in the earlier days of their marriage. Her patience bears fruit when it becomes clear that Ray not only understands her but is able to respond in his own way. Having taken the time to finally connect with her husband, Dorothy finally feels committed to her marriage. By choosing to stay, she finds the freedom that she has always been searching for.

On the surface, the Brinkmans' story seems to have little connection to the rest of the narrative. At the beginning of the novel they are "two people for whom trees mean almost nothing." Their personality traits, however, embody the opposing characteristics of human nature which, Powers suggests, lead us either to care for the environment or destroy it. Dorothy's self-destructive craving for fast-paced excitement and short-term fulfilment is precisely the kind of attitude that has led us to the brink of ecological catastrophe. On the other hand, Ray's patience and ability to wait things out is the approach the novel suggests we need to take to live in harmony with the environment.

The eco-message behind the narrative becomes more evident as trees creep into the cracks of the Brinkmans' relationship, gaining more and more significance. It is no accident that Dorothy finally agrees to marry Ray when he suggests they could mark each anniversary by planting something in their garden. The suggestion is enough to convince Dorothy and also causes her to drive into a linden tree. Significantly, in the rockiest periods of their marriage, the couple forgets to plant anything on their anniversary—a sure sign that at least one of them is neglecting to pay attention to what matters. In another fraught moment of their marriage, we see Ray unable to concentrate on an article proposing that trees should have legal rights, as he knows that Dorothy is with another man.

After Ray's stroke, his physical state is not unlike that of a tree. He lives, he breathes, but there is little outward sign of sentience in his paralyzed expression and garbled attempts to speak. Initially, Dorothy speaks to him to fill the silences and retain a sense of normalcy. A crucial turning point comes, however, when Dorothy reads a crossword clue out to Ray. Hours later, Ray gestures for a pen and scribbles down the word "Releaf." His response shows that he is not only fully sentient, but sharp enough to work out a cryptic clue. The definition of the word he writes, with its link to trees and growth, also offers the promise of regeneration.

With the knowledge that Ray understands her, Dorothy quiets the restless side of her soul to engage in slow and meaningful communication with her husband—the equivalent of listening to trees. Much of this communication is about the trees in their garden, as Dorothy takes the time to identify each one. Her research reveals that their favourite tree is one of the last remaining mature American chestnuts in the country. Now aware of the benefits of reforesting even a small area of land, Dorothy ignores complaints from the neighbours and the city and lets the garden grow wild. Naming it, "the Brinkman Woodlands Restoration Project," the couple see the garden as their legacy to the next generation. As their narrative reaches its conclusion, Ray dies. The story leaves Dorothy bereaved but purposeful as she continues to fight for the right to keep her small patch of wilderness.

Douglas Pavlicek

At the beginning of his story, Douglas is an orphaned lost soul. Lonely and directionless, he bounces from one place and job to the next, searching for something that will give him purpose.

At the age of nineteen, Douglas enrols in the Stanford Prison Experiment—a controversial psychological study where young men were paid to become either prisoners or guards in a simulated prison setting. As Prisoner 571 in this short experiment, Douglas learns a great deal about human nature. Observing the brutal behaviour of the "guards," he sees how easily people fall into prescribed roles. Failings in his own character are also exposed when—along with the other prisoners—Douglas chooses not to give up his blanket for the night, even when it would secure the release of a fellow prisoner from solitary confinement. The experiment leaves Douglas with a horror of imprisonment and the nagging sense that he should have been a better man.

With the naivety of Forrest Gump, Douglas then blunders into another significant moment in 1970s history—the Vietnam War. Prompted to enlist by a vague sense that he can make a difference, he becomes an Air Force loadmaster. His time in the Armed Forces comes to an end when his plane is shot from the sky and his life is saved by the branches of a gigantic fig tree. By this time, he has witnessed not only the loss of human life, but also the

48

obliteration of plants and trees by Agent Orange.

Honourably discharged from the Air Force with a permanently damaged leg, Douglas is older and wiser but still lacks purpose. Although his life has been miraculously saved by a tree, he does not know why. Roaming around the USA, his epiphany unexpectedly comes when he stops for a comfort break. Stepping into some apparently dense woodland at the side of the road, he realizes that the trees are nothing more than a "beauty strip"—an optical illusion of forest concealing vast stretches of land where all the trees have been felled. In a scene which echoes his aerial survey of the effects of Agent Orange, Douglas hires a plane to see the full extent of deforestation.

Having found his purpose, Douglas devotes the next four years of his life to planting saplings. The backbreaking work makes him feel as if he is making a difference, until he discovers that planting these saplings legally allows the timber companies to cut down even more old-growth forest.

Drifting to Portland, Douglas has no clear plans. He is driven to spur-of-the-moment activism, however, when he sees city employees preparing to cut down Ponderosa pines before the agreed hearing. Finding himself in the right place at the right time, he instinctively tries to protect the trees by climbing one of them. The trees are cut down anyway, and Douglas receives a suspended sentence, but his path to activism is firmly set. Revisiting the stumps to draw attention to the city's crime, he meets Mimi.

Douglas's attraction to Mimi both strengthens and complicates his purpose. At first, it is he who encourages her to join him in deforestation protests. Soon, however, she becomes an essential part of his motivation. After Olivia's death, despite the dangers of being seen together, Douglas clings to Mimi until she unequivocally tells him that he must not contact her again.

Without Mimi, Douglas once again drifts into a purposeless life. While working in Montana as the out-of-season caretaker of an old mining town, he processes his experiences as an activist by writing a journal. By calling this memoir a "Manifesto of Failure," Douglas indicates that he has come to view his protesting days as a waste of time. Once again, however, a tree saves his life when he falls from a snowy mountain ridge. Lying in the snow, he receives a message from Olivia who reminds him that his work is not yet done.

Readers never discover whether Douglas would have answered

this call to action from Olivia. Instead, he is arrested by the FBI after he offers a bed to a young woman for the night and she reads his memoir. His arrest prompts a sense of déjà vu, reminding Douglas of his time as Prisoner 571. By now, however, he is a changed person and makes different decisions to those he made in the Stanford Prison Experiment. While previously he refused to betray the leaders of the prison rebellion, this time he cuts a deal for a lighter sentence by exposing Adam as a fellow activist. Consequently, instead of life imprisonment he receives a seven-year sentence in a medium-security prison with eligibility for early parole.

While Douglas's betrayal of Adam serves his own interests, it becomes clear that his main motivation is to protect Mimi's identity. He justifies his actions by telling himself that Adam was more of an observer than a fully-fledged member of the group. Nevertheless, Douglas feels guilty when Adam receives the life sentence that he has avoided. As his narrative comes to a close, he is listening to an audio course on dendrology in his cell, narrated by Patricia Westerford. The undiagnosed lump in his side suggests that he may not see his seven-year sentence to its end.

Neelay Mehta

When Neelay's character is introduced in the novel it is not immediately obvious how his story fits into the narrative. An Indian American, born in California, he is a computer whiz kid, obsessed with the potential of the digital rather than the natural world. Soon enough, however, Neelay has a life-changing encounter with a tree when he falls from an oak and is left paralyzed.

Neelay's disability dramatically limits his future horizons. He is no longer able to go hiking with his father and feels grotesque and unlovable. As a result, he becomes increasingly hermit-like and lonely. On the other hand, the limiting of his physical and social life enables Neelay to immerse himself in creating virtual worlds. Falling from the oak is shown to both break and make him.

Trees also play a part in Neelay's first successful computer games which are set on other planets. The inspiration for the weird and wonderful species he creates in these worlds comes from the outlandishly exotic imported trees he sees on Stanford campus.

From this point, consulting trees for guidance becomes a habit for him. Whenever he has an important decision to make about his ever-expanding business he communes with trees with varying degrees of success. Even the name of his company—Sempervirens—is inspired by the Latin name for a giant redwood he once saw with his father.

Neelay's fascination with the natural world prompts him to try to recreate its richness and diversity within a new computer game—*Mastery*. In this virtual world (seemingly a cross between *SimCity* and *Minecraft*), players emerge on an Earth untouched by mankind and can make of it what they will. Hugely addictive and successful, the game makes Neelay a Silicon Valley millionaire many times over. As time goes on, however, Neelay realizes that, instead of being a haven from the real world, *Mastery* has come to emulate it. The obsession of its players with development and consumption means that new continents and infinite resources must be created to keep up with demand. Dismayed with this turn of events (and inspired by reading *The Secret Forest*), Neelay raises the "Midas problem" with his team, suggesting that they change the way the game works. Instead of the current model, players would be presented with just one, non-expandable Earth and limited resources. The challenge of the game would be to learn what the world needed from you as a player to help it flourish. While Neelay is greatly excited at the prospect, his team fail to share his enthusiasm, unwilling to jeopardize the game's profitability. They vote unanimously against him.

Unable to reverse the desecration of *Mastery*, Neelay moves on to a new, even more ambitious project. His work leads to the creation of digital entities called "Learners" who gather and analyze information on the natural world. The ultimate aim of this work is to discover what the planet needs from humans. Although Neelay knows he will not live long enough to see the project's fruition, he feels satisfied that he has helped to develop it.

Patricia Westerford

Of all the main characters in the novel, Patricia Westerford has the greatest affinity with trees. As a child, her hearing and speech impairments mean she is more comfortable immersed in nature than hanging around with her peers. Inheriting a love of botany from her father, she spends her time quietly and patiently observing forest life.

By the time Patricia arrives at university, she is already driven by a strong sense of vocation (earning her the nickname "Plant-Patty"). This takes her to Forestry School as a graduate but here she discovers that she disagrees with accepted thought on how best to manage forests. Patricia dislikes the emphasis on fast-growing trees as it limits biodiversity. She also disagrees with the theory that the forest floor should be managed by clearing dead trees—knowing from her observations that they play a vital role in the life cycles of other creatures. Patricia's unique approach to the field is also demonstrated in her doctoral thesis. In this she puts forward the radical theory that trees communicate with each other through complex airborne signals. When Patricia's research is published in a journal it causes a stir, receiving favourable attention, even from the popular press. Shortly afterwards, however, three male dendrologists publicly scorn her findings, effectively convincing the rest of the world that Patricia's research is nonsense.

The public ridicule of her work has a devastating effect on Patricia. Discredited as an academic, she decides to commit suicide by eating a deadly fungus she has found in the forest. Her last-minute decision to live (just as the fork reaches her lips) marks a crucial turning point for her. At this moment she determines that she will never let the opinion of other people influence her decisions. She takes a job as a wilderness ranger and then, joining a woodland research team, she begins to write *The Secret Forest*—a book which conveys the many miraculous things she has discovered about the lives of trees. In the meantime, out in the world, the findings of her early research are vindicated and built upon by other scientists.

Despite her liking for solitude, Patricia finds that she enjoys working with like-minded colleagues in a research team. A friendship with the research station manager, Dennis Ward, evolves into an unconventional marriage. Instinctively understanding that Patricia needs time and space to work, Dennis proves to be the ideal "wife," living several miles away but providing her with emotional support and regular meals.

Patricia would be happy to remain living a simple life, immersed in nature, for the rest of her days. When *The Secret Forest* becomes a huge bestseller, however, she must choose between staying in her comfort zone or becoming an ambassador for trees and their cause. She bravely chooses the latter, travelling around the globe and forcing herself to overcome her aversion to public speaking. Her mission is to change the way that trees are perceived and drum up support for her new project—a seed bank to preserve the world's remaining tree species.

In many respects, Patricia and Richard Powers share the same aims in *The Overstory*. Both want to persuade their audience to view trees as sentient life givers rather than commodities. Both also emphasize the pressing need for humans to take action before we completely destroy the world's forests. Powers uses Patricia's role as a scientist to convey facts and data to back up these arguments. When Patricia travels around the world collecting specimens for her seed bank, it provides the author with an opportunity to illustrate that the issue of deforestation is a global one. In describing the challenges Patricia faces in conveying her message, the author acknowledges the issues he also had to confront in writing the novel. Patricia recognizes that, to convey the scale of the deforestation crisis, she needs to provide facts and figures. Overdoing this statistical information, however, can be overwhelming for her audiences— "Too many zeros: their eyes glaze over. She must shepherd them back over that ultrafine line between numbness and awe." It is left for readers to judge whether the author succeeds in finding this balance.

After chronicling her astonishing achievements, Powers brings Patricia's story to a close in a tantalizingly uncertain way. Invited to speak at an environmental conference on repairing the planet, Patricia agonizes over what to say. In the end, her talk focuses on the concept that, by continuing the rapid rate of deforestation, the human race is effectively committing suicide. In conclusion, she bleakly suggests that the best thing that people can do for the planet is to remove themselves from it. Raising a glass containing an apparently deadly solution collected from trees, it seems that she is about to drink. At this moment, the author splits the narrative into two possibilities—Patricia dramatically commits suicide in front of the audience, or she offers up a toast to "unsuicide" and throws the solution into the crowd. Readers are left to decide which strategy Patricia took. By leaving this question open, Powers places his readers in a moral predicament. Despite Patricia's argument that she is old and has achieved as much as she can, few readers would want to imagine that she dies. On the other hand, we are forced to consider whether her suicide would make the most persuasive point to the rest of the world.

Regardless of Patricia's final fate, she is shown to leave an impressive legacy. Although she does not meet the other main characters they read, and are deeply influenced by, *The Secret Forest*. Meanwhile, the image of the frozen specimens in her seed bank "all waiting for their DNA to awaken" offers a welcome glimmer of hope for the future.

Olivia Vandergriff

At the beginning of the novel, 25-year-old Olivia Vandergriff seems an unlikely eco-heroine. Significantly, she is too self-absorbed to notice the extraordinary tree that stands outside her student house. Instead, freshly divorced from a sex and drug-fuelled marriage, she celebrates her freedom by stealing her housemates' beer and getting high. Her careless life comes to a dramatic end when she touches her lamp switch with a wet hand and is electrocuted.

Olivia's physical resurrection after her brief death also involves a transformation of her spirit. When she revives, she is a completely different person, convinced, for the first time, that her life has real purpose. To find out just what that purpose is, she focuses on the voices of the "beings of light" who begin to speak to her. In a leap of faith, Olivia follows their instructions, abandoning her undergraduate course in actuarial science (along with most of her possessions) and driving towards the Midwest. The purpose of her mission becomes clear when she sees a TV broadcast showing eco-warriors in Solace, California, protesting against the felling of ancient redwood trees. From that moment, Olivia dedicates her life to fighting deforestation.

Olivia (or Maidenhair, as she becomes) has a bewitching effect on the characters she comes into contact with—an impact undeniably enhanced by the fact that she is "gorgeous." Nick, Adam and Mimi all fall in love with her to some degree. The same goes for some of the loggers who unsuccessfully try to persuade her to end her extended tree squat in the giant redwood, Mimas. Olivia's real magnetic power, however, comes from her fearlessness and unwavering belief in her cause. Faced with her conviction, it becomes possible for the other characters to believe in the words tattooed across her shoulder blade—"A change is gonna come."

Given Olivia's absolute certainty that her mission will turn out well, it comes as a shock when she is killed by an explosion during the group's increasingly extreme attacks on logging company property. In the aftermath of her death, the group splits and the other characters are left questioning whether their actions have achieved anything. Olivia does, however, continue to motivate the characters after she is gone. It is her memory that finally prompts a devastated Nick to continue his activism through art. Meanwhile, when Douglas reaches the point where he almost gives up on life (after falling from a mountain ridge) she appears to him and tells him that his work is not done.

Throughout the novel, Olivia's character is imbued with mystical qualities. Compared to a "dryad" and "Joan of Arc", she often seems more goddess-like than human. The air of mystery that surrounds her character is deepened by certain cryptic references in the novel that seem to suggest she may be Ray and Dorothy's daughter. Early on in their story, we learn that Ray and Dorothy's inability to conceive is a source of great sadness to them. We also learn, however, that Olivia's father is an intellectual property lawyer—an odd coincidence, as this is also Ray's profession. Years later, as the Brinkmans admire the mature chestnut tree in the garden, Ray refers to planting the seedling with their daughter. He goes on to describe her, and in her mind's eye Dorothy sees their daughter's various stages of development—from the age of six, when she plants the sapling with her father, to the twenty-year-old who visits from college with "a horrible new baroque tattoo on her left shoulder." Whether these are real memories, or imaginings is not entirely clear. Is Olivia the daughter the Brinkmans would have liked to have had, or their flesh and blood child, now lost? Readers are left to make up their own minds.

The Trees

While the nine human protagonists provide the "understory" of the novel, we cannot forget that trees are its "overstory"—the real stars of the show. Richard Powers admits that, ideally, he would have liked to have written the entire novel from the perspective of trees.

In the end, however, he felt that this would be beyond his own "power as a novelist and ... probably ... beyond the imaginative power of identification of most readers." Instead, he does the next best thing, bringing the miraculous nature of trees to life through his prose.

Even the trees with the smallest cameo roles have distinct personalities in the novel thanks to Powers's use of personification and anthropomorphism. Oaks "wave prophecies" and hawthorns "laugh," while humans consistently fail to understand what they are saying. To add to this effect, parallels are drawn between tree behaviour and our own— the way they communicate with one another, help one another in crises, migrate, and sacrifice themselves for their children.

Lovingly detailing the quirks of individual species—the "spiny fruits" of chinquapin, the "blood-red clusters" of rowans, Powers also draws attention to the ways in which trees surpass humans— their longevity, the myriad ways in which they reproduce, and the way they sustain other life without ever taking it. Yet, despite all this, we continue to treat trees as inanimate commodities. This point is neatly illustrated when Patricia takes the time to thank a cedar "for the baskets and boxes ... the capes and hats and skirts ... The cradles. The beds. The diapers. Canoes. Paddles, harpoons, and nets. Poles, logs, posts ..."—and the list goes on. Trees give us so much but what, the author asks, do we give back?

Among the hundreds of trees mentioned in the novel, the births and deaths of particular individuals are foregrounded. These are the trees that play pivotal roles in the lives of the main characters. The Hoel Chestnut is a hardy pioneer like the Norwegian who initially plants it. Transplanted from its native territory in New York to Iowa, the tree continues to thrive when most American chestnut trees have been wiped out by blight. It also survives several generations of the Hoel family, quietly persisting through births, deaths, marriages and divorces, as well as momentous national events—the Depression, two World Wars, etc. During this time, photographing the tree gives members of each successive generation a sense of purpose. After seeing things out until Nick (the last survivor of his line) must leave the family home, the chestnut finally gives in to blight, marking the end of an era. When Nick returns, years later, the tree has been cut down, but new chestnut shoots spring from its stump. Nick initially takes this as a sign of hope until he realizes that the shoots will also carry the blight.

The Ma mulberry also plays a pivotal role in the lives of the family who choose to plant it. Transplanted from China to a new life in the USA, Winston Ma plants a mulberry in his backyard as a reminder of his heritage (mulberry leaves are a favourite food of silkworms and his family's fortune was made from silk plantations). The tree provides a shady spot for Winston's three daughters to breakfast under in the summer. When, years later, it succumbs to disease, this coincides with devastating events in the Mas' lives. The mulberry's slow death reflects the gradual deterioration of the mind of Winston's wife, Charlotte, who has early onset dementia. Meanwhile, Winston sees the demise of the tree as a sign that he has nothing left to achieve. His decision to kill himself under the mulberry highlights the way he feels his fate and that of the tree are intertwined. This connection is further emphasized by the fact that his brains splatter in precisely the spots where the dark red fruits of the tree usually fall.

The Appich trees are even more specifically attached to the identity of the family who plants them. As a different species is planted in the garden to commemorate the birth of each child, every one of the Appich children identifies themselves with a particular tree. As a child, Adam firmly believes that the type of tree they are assigned will define who they become. Later, with the more cynical perspective of a psychologist, he concludes that the process pre-conditioned the evolution of their characters. Whatever the truth of the matter, the Appich siblings grow to resemble their trees. Like the leaves of his maple, socially awkward Adam turns red easily. His baby brother, Charles, grows just like the black walnut—tall, with beautifully grained wood, rock-hard nuts, and roots which poison "the ground beneath itself so nothing else can grow" (in other words, a handsome bully). Most significantly, after Leigh's tree dies of Dutch elm disease, she is abducted and never seen again—a tragic event which ultimately tears apart the family.

The chestnut tree in the Brinkmans' garden—barely noticed by the couple in the more troubled years of their marriage—takes on greater significance to both of them in their later years. Like the Hoel Chestnut, it has grown beyond its native area, escaping disease. This makes it one of the last remaining mature chestnuts in the country. The tree comes to represent the way that Dorothy and Ray's relationship has endured and grown. For the Brinkmans, the chestnut is a sign of hope for the future and becomes synonymous with the daughter they may or may not have had.

Of all the trees in the novel, Mimas is the only one to be given a name. A giant from Greek mythology, Mimas was the son of Gaia (Mother Earth). This name nicely reflects the characteristics of the Californian redwood, which is ancient, monumental in size, and inspires such awe in the characters that they feel as if they are confronting a "divinity." The act of naming the redwood also transforms Mimas from an "it" to a "he", emphasizing the fact that he is a sentient life form. Just as farmers do not tend to name livestock destined for slaughter, the activists hope that by naming Mimas they will make it more difficult for the loggers to cut him down.

When volunteers are required to squat in Mimas to prevent him from being felled, Olivia feels as if she has discovered her true purpose. Nick accompanies her, and in the intimate world of Mimas's branches, the couple learns to slow down to the pace of tree life. Despite their best efforts, Olivia and Nick are only able to offer Mimas a temporary reprieve from the loggers. When they are arrested and taken into police custody, Mimas and all the surrounding redwoods are felled. The image of his severed stump (still taller than Olivia) brings home the scale of the loss.

THEMES & IMAGERY

The Overstory

The title of the novel, interpreted literally, describes a forest canopy. The overstory is formed by the largest treetops which create the conditions for all the smaller life forms that live below. The author's choice of title brilliantly encapsulates both his subject matter and themes. This is not a novel about humans where trees provide the scenic background—trees are the main story. This, unusually, makes the human characters of the novel "the understory"—just another species on the forest floor relying on the life-giving generosity of trees.

Roots

The structure and much of the imagery in *The Overstory* centres upon roots. The interconnected nature of roots reflects the fact that all living things are linked. The vast network of invisible roots underground comes to represent the many intricate and often unknowable ways in which living things depend upon one another within ecosystems. Take away the roots and that fine balance is destroyed.

When several of the protagonists in the novel unite, the structure of a root system is echoed. Beginning the novel as lone individuals, Olivia, Nick, Douglas and Mimi join forces when they discover that they share the "vocation" of saving old-growth forests. Even Patricia, with her liking for solitude, is surprised to find she enjoys working with research colleagues in "one great symbiotic association." In both cases, the groups are shown to achieve more together than they could alone.

Activism

In *The Overstory*, Richard Powers makes no secret of his belief that, given the severity of our current ecological crisis, public protest and activism is necessary. On more than one occasion, characters remind us of the positive social changes that would not have taken place without it—votes for women, the abolition of slavery, etc. The same argument is also made when Mimi points out that "Yesterday's political criminals are on today's postage stamps!" Establishing this point, the novel then examines what actions can be justified in the name of activism.

In their early days of protesting, Olivia and Nick join an environmental group committed to non-violent activism, led by the out-and-out pacifist, Mother N. Mimi and Douglas also begin protesting peacefully. In both cases, protest involves putting their bodies in the way of the logging industry. Olivia and Nick squat in a Californian redwood to stop it being felled while Mimi and Douglas climb or handcuff themselves to trees.

Reading Powers's descriptions of these logging protests, there can be little doubt that the author sympathizes with the motivations of his activist characters. He also ensures that readers understand why his protagonists graduate from this kind of non-violent resistance to eco-terrorism. In a series of harrowing scenes (several loosely based on real events) he shows non-violent protesters brutalized in different ways. Activists are dragged along by the vehicles they have chained themselves to, Olivia and Nick are almost knocked out of Mimas by a helicopter, and a helpless Douglas is stripped and sprayed in the groin with pepper spray after dropping the key to his handcuffs. Perhaps the most shocking of these scenes is the one in which police officers methodically apply a solution of concentrated pepper to the eyes of screaming handcuffed protesters with Q-tips. Witnessing this happening to Mimi, Douglas describes her as being "Gangbanged in the eyes by three guys", drawing a parallel with rape.

By the time they conclude that non-violent protest is a "luxury," Douglas and Mimi bear permanent physical injuries. Mimi is left with a disfiguring facial scar while Douglas's limp becomes even more pronounced after a digger fractures his leg. Olivia and Nick, meanwhile, tried peaceable methods to save Mimas and failed. Powers makes it clear that his characters have been pushed to extremes by a system that does not play fair. Both the logging industry and police officers are depicted as disregarding the safety of protesters and their human rights. The police force fails to show up when protesters are being harmed, use unwarranted force when they arrest them and hold them in custody for longer than is legal. There is also more than a suggestion of police corruption when the news breaks that the peace-loving Mother N has been killed by explosives which, the police claim, she planned to use for terrorism. Taking all this into account, it is not difficult to see why the activists decide to turn to more aggressive forms of protest. Empathizing with their actions is made easier still by the fact that they do not harm innocent people in the process. In the end, Olivia is the only person to be injured by their use of explosives. Her death, however, raises the question of how we would feel about their actions if the group had accidentally killed someone other than one of their own? In the end, these are questions for the reader to decide.

While the novel invites sympathy for the activists' motivations, it raises questions about how much they achieve. When Douglas writes a memoir of his time as an activist, he significantly calls it his "Manifesto of Failure," reflecting the fact that their actions changed very little in the long-term. Despite Olivia and Nick's valiant tree squat, Mimas is still cut down, and other protests are shown to be little more than inconveniences for the timber companies who quickly resume business as usual. Even the sacrifice of Olivia's death seems to be rendered pointless when the message of Nick's graffiti, left at the scene, is misinterpreted and the press concludes she was killed by a madman. In the end, it is the actions of other protagonists that are shown to have a more long-term impact (Patricia's books and seed bank, and Neelay's Learners.) Perhaps of all the activists, it is Adam—the least consistent of the group—who goes on to make the most impact on public opinion. By the sheer length of his prison sentence, he garners attention, at least for a while, as the man who gave everything up for trees.

Time & Patience

Throughout *The Overstory* there is a contrast between the human experience of time and time as experienced by trees. Without the interference of humans, trees have longer life spans and existed long before the human race. Tree history, the author suggests, is on such a different scale to human history that it is hard for us to even grasp the concept.

The contrast between tree and human time is beautifully conveyed through the story of the Hoel family. The Hoel Chestnut, planted by Nick's great-great-great-grandfather, survives several generations of Hoel family dramas. It continues to grow, silently and invisibly, regardless of two world wars, the Depression and the introduction of new farming technology —all of this happening "in a couple of new fissures, an inch of added rings." When John Hoel begins photographing the chestnut each month, he cannot articulate what prompts him to begin the project. Nor can successive generations say exactly what it is that compels them to continue it. What becomes clear to the reader is that the Hoels are trying to capture the sense of human transience they feel in the presence of this great tree. This idea is echoed later in the novel when Nick sleeps on the huge stump of Mimas after the giant redwood has been felled. Through his body, Nick becomes aware of the sheer scale of Mimas's life—"his head … near the ring laid down the year Charlemagne died. Somewhere underneath his coccyx, Columbus." Similarly, when Adam is found guilty of domestic terrorism, he sees his two consecutive 70 year sentences from the perspective of tree years. "The leniency shocks him. He thinks: *A black willow plus a wild cherry*. He was thinking Oak."

One of the great virtues of trees is shown to be their patience. This quality is contrasted with the impatience of the human race as a whole. The frantic "rate of human desire" is, the novel suggests, behind the devastating rate of deforestation. Our urge to have a limitless supply of timber in the present moment prevents us from thinking about the long-term cost. If only, Powers implies, we could be more like trees and learn to play the long game instead of slavishly satisfying our short-term desires.

When Neelay is a child, his father tells him that "Patience is the maker of all good things," and this becomes an important lesson in the novel. Some of the protagonists possess patience naturally, doggedly devoting themselves to goals which seem pointless to others. Patricia, for example is never happier than when conducting repetitive observation and research. The Hoel family also embody this characteristic, as generation after generation faithfully photograph a tree, while Nick devotes a decade to unsaleable tree art. There are other characters who must learn patience. We see this in Olivia's transformation from party girl to tree-sitter. Also, in Dorothy's U-turn, from serial adulterer to carer for her unerringly patient husband, Ray.

In some cases, the projects that the characters embark on are so long-term that they will not live to see their fruition. This is the case with Patricia's seed bank and Neelay's creation of a tree-interpreting artificial intelligence. Both characters possess enough vision, however, to foresee the benefits of the end result. In doing so, they display a world view that, the novel suggests, we would all do well to adopt. As Patricia argues, "if you want next century soil, if you want pure water, if you want variety and health, ... then be patient and let the forest give slowly."

Whether humans are capable of emulating the patience of trees remains to be seen. In his examination of time, however, the author reminds us that trees were here long before we climbed down from them and, if they can survive our presence, may continue on Earth long after we are gone.

Suicide/ Unsuicide

Even as a child, Adam is aware that there is something essentially wrong with human nature. Observing other peoples' self-destructive tendencies, he grimly concludes that "Humankind is deeply ill," and "the species won't last long." Patricia sees this same wilful drive towards annihilation in the way we treat our environment. She points out that, although human life depends upon the existence of trees, we continue to cut down the small percentage of remaining old-growth forest without accounting for the consequences. Asked to advise on the best thing a person can do to save the planet at an environmental conference, she suggests committing collective suicide—a recommendation she may or may not follow through with herself.

In *The Overstory*, the end of mankind is anticipated with a certain amount of optimism. Patricia is not the only character to believe that human extinction may be the best solution to the threats facing the natural world. Both Douglas and Winston Ma express a hopeful belief that trees and animals will outlive us. Readers are, therefore, left to consider whether it might be better if we all died.

Happily, the novel offers an alternative option which could allow for the survival of both trees and people. This is "unsuicide"—a proposition which Patricia toasts in the second version of her conference speech. To commit unsuicide, Patricia suggests, humans would have to take less and give more, becoming more quietly receptive to what our environment requires from us. This philosophy is summed up when Nick spells out the word "STILL" on the forest floor in dead timber. Playing on the double meaning of the word, Nick's art suggests that in order to endure (i.e. *still* exist), we need to acquire the skill of stillness, living life at a slower pace.

Plant-blindness

While Patricia sees plants in all their miraculous glory, her father warns her that most people are "Plant-blind." This is demonstrated in the Appich household (despite their tree-planting ceremonies) when only Adam notices the demise of his sister's elm tree.

Throughout *The Overstory* the author suggests that this inability to really see the natural world is at the heart of humanity's problem. Our sense of disconnection from our natural surroundings leads us to see trees as commodities rather than an essential part of our ecosystem. It is also the cause of humanity's deep-seated sense of alienation and loneliness.

Enlightenment

Enlightenment is presented as the solution to plant blindness. This joyful state of being is depicted on the ancient Chinese scroll Mimi inherits from her father. Winston Ma explains the concept of enlightenment to Mimi as, "human beings, so small. And life, so very big." At the time, Mimi cannot understand why the three old men depicted on the scroll are so happy at this realization. Later, however, along with the other main characters, she is to experience her own moment of enlightenment when she begins to feel a deep connection with trees. Only when the protagonists experience this oneness with the natural world can they truly connect with themselves and other people.

Communication

One of the central concerns of *The Overstory* is the way that humans so often fail to meaningfully connect with their surroundings. This point is illustrated through the theme of communication.

As children, Adam and Patricia both find conventional social communication difficult. Adam's autistic tendencies make the whole field of social interaction challenging for him, while Patricia has hearing and speech impairments. These very social failings, however, make them more sensitive to silent forms of communication that other people are oblivious to. Adam becomes aware of the silent way in which ants signal to one another, and Patricia becomes convinced of the communicative abilities of trees.

Later in the novel, Mimi discovers that she has developed a gift for silent communication. Looking into Olivia's eyes as she dies, Mimi hears the other woman's thoughts. This discovery leads her to become an unconventional yet highly effective therapist. Her technique involves holding a client's gaze and conducting a silent dialogue with them. Mimi's ability to hold conversations without either person speaking is mirrored in the Brinkmans' relationship after Ray has a stroke. Over time, Dorothy learns to read her husband's thoughts and feelings despite few clues from his paralyzed face.

For the characters, understanding these silent means of communication involves patience and an opening up of the self—a blocking out of the chatter of the outside world and a focus on the deeper and more meaningful. This attentive type of listening is, the author suggests, the only way to tune in to what the natural world is saying to us.

Ownership/ Property

Concepts of property and ownership lie at the heart of the conflict in the Brinkmans' troubled marriage. Dorothy has issues with her husband's choice of career (as an intellectual property lawyer) and is also angered by the belief that Ray considers her to be his property. This storyline highlights a larger point Powers makes in the novel about the way humans treat the environment in general, and trees in particular. The author suggests that becoming more environmentally aware involves not just managing our resources better but questioning whether those resources really belong to us in the first place.

Throughout the novel, Powers depicts a society that knows the price of everything and the value of nothing. Nick literally cannot give away his tree artwork, as people do not see its value. Meanwhile, an essential part of Olivia's spiritual transformation is abandoning her undergraduate course in actuarial science. By giving up a field of study which calculates "the cash value of death," she can concentrate on the true value of the lives of trees. Most people, however, continue to see trees as commodities to make everything from shampoo to shoe polish. As Douglas succinctly says, they are the "Cheapest priceless stuff that ever has been."

Critiquing the consumerist spirit that makes us assume all living things are our property, the author shows his enlightened characters shaking off attachments to material possessions. When he leaves his family home Nick keeps nothing, while Olivia embarks on her mission with just the bare necessities. Non-materialistic Patricia is happiest living in a cabin in the woods with none of the conveniences of modern life.

When it comes to rejecting commodity culture, *The Overstory*'s protagonists are extreme role models to aspire to. In reality, few of us are likely to give up our worldly possessions and go off-grid. In a couple of memorable statements from his characters, however, Powers suggests more realistic goals for his readers. Nick's simple statement, "We need to get smarter about what we need" urges us to think more deeply about the commodities we really require. Meanwhile, Patricia suggests a new way to think about the source of our wood-derived goods—"My simple rule of thumb … is this: when you cut down a tree, what you make from it should be at least as miraculous as what you cut down."

In the Brinkmans' story, Ray not only comes to question the concept of trees as property but concludes that they should have similar legal rights to humans. If this seems a step too far to be credible, readers are reminded that, in recent history, women and African Americans have "all gone from property to personhood."

Mastery

When Neelay creates the computer game *Mastery*, he combines his fascination with the natural and the digital worlds. Determined to capture the richness and diversity found in nature, he makes a virtual world where players emerge in an unspoiled area of Earth and can do with it as they please.

Mastery is initially intended to be like the real world only better. Here, players can retreat to an Earth as it once was before man began destroying his environment. The irony is that, once the game becomes popular, its players begin to ruin it in exactly the same way, through over-development and pointless overconsumption. *Mastery* comes to symbolize the insatiable human desire for dominion over all living things.

Religious Symbolism

References to religion and spirituality abound in *The Overstory*. Many of the allusions are to ancient forms of spirituality such as Greek myth, paganism, Buddhism, and Native American religions. Significantly, these are all belief systems in which man's relationship with the natural world is an important element. By featuring these faiths, Powers suggests that the Western world is poorer for having forgotten this connection. This point is nicely illustrated at the end of the novel when a Native American reminds Nick that his people have known for centuries that trees can communicate.

As well as highlighting the beliefs of these more pantheistic religions, Powers makes liberal use of traditional Christian symbolism in the novel. Olivia, in particular, is often presented as a saintly or even Christ-like figure. Her miraculous return to life after electrocution echoes Lazarus's return from the dead and, of course, the resurrection of Jesus. Even more specific in its use of religious imagery is Olivia's second death scene. In a reproduction of a "pietà" (the image of the Virgin Mary with the body of Christ), Mimi cradles Olivia's head in her dying moments. Like Jesus Christ, Olivia is a charismatic leader bearing an important message from above, who eventually sacrifices herself for the cause. Nick, Mimi, Douglas and Adam are the disciples tasked with continuing to spread the word once she has gone.

While Olivia gives up her life for her beliefs, her fellow protagonists also sacrifice a great deal to further their cause. When Nick first awakens to the plight of trees, he dreams that branches are growing from wounds on his palms—wounds similar to

Christ's stigmata. After Douglas has suffered the pain and humiliation of having his genitalia doused with pepper spray, the police "carry him down from the tree like Jesus from the cross." Douglas's spiritual journey is not, however, as simple as converting from sinner to saint. Later in the novel he is compared to Judas when he betrays Adam to the police (walking past a Judas tree as he records their conversation).

Biblical comparisons are not just confined to the non-activist characters in the novel. When Patricia decides to attempt to save the world's remaining tree species by starting a seed bank, Dennis compares the project to Noah's ark. Neelay, meanwhile, brings to mind a disappointed God when he realizes that players have ruined the perfect world he created in *Mastery*.

Overall, the proliferation of Christian symbolism gives the novel an epic feel. Individual stories take on the quality of parables, underlining the seriousness of the characters' cause. In using this imagery, the author seems to suggest that if any mission is sacred it is surely the battle to save what remains of the world's forests.

Metamorphosis

Metamorphosis is defined in the dictionary as "a change of the form or nature of a thing or person into a completely different one." In *The Overstory*, however, Richard Powers, puts a slightly different slant on it. While metamorphosis is a recurring theme in the novel, it is not represented as a dramatic transformation from one entirely different species to another. Instead, it involves a recognition that the borders between living things are less rigid than we perceive them to be.

From her early days, Patricia is interested in the potential of living things to transform into other living things. As a girl, one of her favourite activities is making animal figures out of debris from the forest floor—twigs, acorns, pinecones etc. Then, as a teenager, she is bewitched by the myths she reads in Ovid's *Metamorphoses*, where people turn into animals, birds, and best of all, trees. Patricia is bewitched by Ovid's classic because it confirms her own view of the world. In her eyes, the division between the world of humans and the natural world (particularly trees) is a fluid one. While the majority of people view trees as inanimate objects, she feels a deep connection with them. As a scientist, Patricia goes on to prove her early hunches, unearthing parallels between tree and human behaviour and names her second book *The New Metamorphosis*. During a trip to the Amazon rainforest, she encounters a being who could have stepped straight out of Ovid's myths—a tree that looks so much like a woman, she initially mistakes it for a sculpture.

This theme is continued in the stories of Nick, Olivia, Mimi, Douglas and Adam. Uniting in an effort to save the country's last old-growth trees, they take on tree names, paint their faces into wild masks and even don animal costumes for one of their protests. By transforming themselves in this way, they affirm their strong sense of connection to the natural world. For Nick and Olivia this transformation goes a step further during the time that they live in the branches of the redwood, Mimas. Dwelling in the overstory, the couple becomes more in touch with their "animal" selves, suddenly more aware of their senses and the workings of their own bodies.

For Neelay, it is the virtual world that provides opportunities for metamorphosis. Frustrated by his physical limitations in the real world, he can "reincarnate" into a body of any age, gender, or race in the computer game *Mastery*. In this context, humans are "a species turning from animal into data."

By illustrating these different types of metamorphoses, *The Overstory* ultimately argues for a transformation of consciousness on the part of the human race. Powers suggests that to preserve what remains of our natural environment, we must begin to recognize that we are part of a wider ecology of living things.

The Bystander Effect

The bystander effect is a proven social phenomenon, first recognized by psychologists in the 1960s. It describes a pattern of social behaviour where individuals are less likely to intervene in an emergency if other people are present. The larger the crowd, the greater the chance that no one will step forward to help. Psychologists have identified a number of factors which go some way to explaining this odd human characteristic. One is that, within a crowd setting, people feel less sense of responsibility and believe that, if intervention is required, someone else will step in. Another is that the presence of other people may interfere with our ability to identify an emergency (i.e. if no one else is panicking then everything must be fine). Perhaps the most powerful factor of all, however, is the human aversion to stepping out of line by going against the behaviour of the group.

In *The Overstory*, we see the bystander effect in action when Professor Rabinowski excuses himself from a lecture, staggers into the hall and has a heart attack without a single student coming to his aid. As psychology students, all those present are aware of the bystander effect, but still they do nothing. Such is the power of social conformity.

During his participation in the Stanford Prison Experiment, Douglas witnesses a similar phenomenon. Despite knowing that they are simply roleplaying, the participants quickly succumb to the power dynamics of the prisoner/guard relationship. When an announcement is made that the prisoners can secure the release of a fellow inmate if just one of them gives up their blanket for the night, no one steps up. Douglas, however, feels so bad about it that he is unable to sleep.

In *The Overstory*, the author makes a convincing case that the bystander effect explains the human attitude to climate change thus far. Despite all evidence to the contrary, we convince ourselves that it cannot be a real crisis because no one else seems to be panicking. Through his characters, Powers demonstrates that going against the tide of this kind of social conformity takes strength and courage. Neelay, Mimi, and Adam are all taught by their parents that fitting in with the crowd is an essential life skill. As the children of immigrants, Mimi and Neelay are encouraged to assimilate. Adam's father, meanwhile, makes it clear that he wishes his son were more "normal."

The potential consequences of resisting the bystander effect are illustrated after Patricia first publishes her theory that trees talk to each other. Crushed by the weight of public ridicule, she is driven to the point of suicide. When she changes her mind at the last moment, however, Patricia decides that she will never again worry about public opinion. Instead, she will embark on the ambitious quest of getting the rest of the world to see things her way.

Significantly, several of the novel's protagonists are outsiders or loners. This demonstrates that it is much easier for individuals to discern the truth when they are not fully immersed in society. To make a difference, the characters must be prepared to go against

70

the crowd, possibly appearing mad or deluded to others. In Olivia's case, this means freely admitting that she takes instructions from voices in her head. This raises interesting questions about society's concepts of sanity. When Nick looks up the definition of schizophrenia, it includes the caveat, "Beliefs should not be considered delusional if they are in keeping with societal norms." In other words, those who go along with the bystander effect will always be considered sane. As Olivia points out, however, "What's crazier? Believing there might be nearby presences we don't know about? Or cutting down the last few ancient redwoods on Earth for decking and shingles?"

The Digital World

In a novel that celebrates the natural world, readers might expect the digital world to be depicted as its natural enemy. Advanced technology is, after all, the product of the kind of progress which has contributed to destroying our planet. As a former computer programmer, however, Powers is able to see this theme in a more nuanced way, teasing out surprising connections between the natural and the digital worlds.

By setting much of the novel in Silicon Valley and the surrounding area, the author shows technology and nature coexisting, side-by-side. In Silicon Valley, technological giants such as Google, and Apple thrive—as well as the computer genius, Neelay Mehta. Close by lie ancient old-growth forests, populated by Californian redwoods that have stood there for hundreds of years.

For Neelay, the natural and the digital worlds are inextricably linked. The first games he creates are inspired by the exotic trees on Stanford campus, and he goes on to name his company Sempervirens (the Latin name for the Californian redwood). The obsessive attention to detail he applies to creating virtual worlds is inspired by a desire to create something as magnificent as the biodiversity on Earth. In describing Neelay's work, Powers highlights the similarities between the growth of roots and branches in trees and the way computer code develops.

Neelay is shown to have lofty ideals when it comes to computer programming but inevitably falls prey to commercialism. Powers establishes a neat parallel between the free games Neelay initially develops and distributes (before turning to the commercial market) and the way we commercially exploit the gifts that trees bestow on us. A similar point is made in describing the way the virtual world of *Mastery* (initially an untouched paradise) becomes corrupted by the greed of its players. It is not technology itself that is at fault here but human nature. The digital world is just another arena for man's capacity for destruction to make its mark.

At the end of the novel, Neelay embarks on an ambitious computer programming project which aims to discover precisely what the planet requires from humans in order to save it. As part of this project, he creates digital entities called "Learners" which, over time, evolve into a "new species." Eventually, we are told, this new form of artificial intelligence will be able to translate between the language of trees and humans.

Could artificial intelligence evolve to save the planet where man has so miserably failed? Powers seems to offer this possibility as one of the glimmers of hope for the future in the novel (the other being Patricia's seed bank). There is also the implied possibility, however, that AI, as a less destructive and more efficient species, may eventually replace humans.

Literature

The Overstory begins with three quotations—one from the American poet and philosopher Ralph Waldo Emerson, one from English environmentalist James Lovelock, and one from Aboriginal Australian Bill Neidjie. Each of the quotations is a reflection on the interconnection between man, trees, and the Earth, setting the tone for the rest of the novel.

Powers's novel is clearly influenced by environmental non-fiction. Patricia Westerford's book *The Secret Forest* bears strong similarities to Peter Wohlleben's *The Hidden Life of Trees*, published in 2016. A German former forester and conservationist, Wohlleben convincingly argues that trees have distinct personalities, live like families, communicate with one another underground, and feel pain.

Clues to Powers's other influences can be found in Patricia's favourite reading matter. The botanist loves the work of John Muir, the naturalist and early environmentalist who campaigned to preserve American forests through the creation of National Parks.

She is also a fan of Thoreau, the nineteenth-century poet and essayist whose philosophies on the natural world reverberate throughout the novel. Anticipating environmentalism before it even existed, Henry David Thoreau had a holistic view of the natural world. Believing in the spiritual benefit of immersing oneself in nature, he felt that too many material trappings got in the way of authentic living. These ideas were encapsulated in his most famous work, *Walden*, which describes his experiences of retreating to a cabin in the woods for two years. Thoreau was a man who loved chestnuts but felt guilty about shaking the tree to bring down its fruits, writing in his journal "it is worse than boorish, it is criminal, to inflict an unnecessary injury on the tree that feeds or shadows us. Old trees are our parents, and our parents' parents, perchance." Even Thoreau's death was linked to his love of trees, as he reputedly died of tuberculosis after an ill-advised decision to count the rings of a tree stump in the rain. It would be difficult to find two writers more closely aligned in their message as the great writer of *Walden* and Richard Powers. Thoreau's spirit infuses *The Overstory*.

As well as non-fictional influences, *The Overstory* teams with references from other literary genres, illustrating the author's love of all kinds of reading matter. In his description of the Hoel family's history, for example, Powers cannot resist slipping in a reference to Walt Whitman, the "poet-nurse" who writes "a leaf of grass is no less than the journey-work of the stars" during the American Civil War. Many of the books referred to neatly tie in with the themes of *The Overstory*. Neelay, for example, reads John Steinbeck's *The Pearl* in American literature (a morality tale about human greed). Patricia's boyfriend at college is a fan of *Moby Dick* (a novel about man versus nature). Meanwhile, on a ranch, Douglas reads *The Complete Nostradamus* and Milton to the horses, thus covering the topics of imminent world disaster and man's loss of paradise.

Often in the novel, reading material has an even deeper significance to the characters involved. In a throwaway line we learn that, shortly before his life-changing accident, Neelay had been studying *A Separate Peace* in American literature class—a novel in which one of the main characters is crippled when he falls out of a tree. Meanwhile, the whole course of the Brinkmans' relationship is charted by significant literary landmarks. Dorothy agrees to date

Ray on the condition that they audition for an amateur production of *Macbeth*. When they are cast as Lady Macbeth and Macduff, this accurately reflects their personalities (Dorothy's fiery and ruthless nature and Ray's dogged reliability). As Macduff is the character who literally brings Birnam Wood to Dunsinane (signalling Macbeth's doom) this also foreshadows the fact that trees will take on great significance in their lives. Later in their relationship we see the Brinkmans returning home from the opening night of *Who's Afraid of Virginia Woolf*. Dorothy's drunken bickering echoes the behaviour of Martha in Edward Albee's play, who has come to bitterly resent her husband. After Ray has a stroke, Dorothy reads Tolstoy's *Anna Karenina* to her husband—a novel with a restless and adulterous heroine. Ray, looking out into the backyard echoes the novel's famous first line ("All happy families are alike; each unhappy family is unhappy in its own way") when he reflects "Civilized yards are all alike. Every wild yard is wild in its own way."

Not content with featuring a whole range of literature, *The Overstory* debates the purpose of fiction as a whole. When Adam reads a novel "about privileged people having trouble getting along with each other in exotic locations," he ends up throwing it against the wall. Here, Powers takes the opportunity to express his belief that, in this era of crisis, literary fiction that focuses on the navel-gazing of its characters has become redundant. Serious novelists, the author believes, should be tackling bigger issues.

Significantly, Ray, the most likable of the Brinkmans, favours non-fiction, while the self-indulgent Dorothy likes fiction where the heroines remind her of herself. After his stroke, Ray (now a captive audience) is converted to the novels Dorothy reads to him while seeing the inherent flaw in them all—they suggest that "*character*—is all that matters in the end. It's a child's creed, of course … to confuse a satisfying story with a meaningful one." There is undeniable truth in the novel's argument that people like fiction because it is tidier and more palatable than real life and reflects our own preoccupations. To suggest that the enjoyment we get from these stories is "childish," however, is a bold statement indeed—and one that runs the risk of irritating the very novel-loving readers who have bought *The Overstory*.

Powers is too intelligent a writer not to appreciate the obvious paradox in a novel which critiques the novel as a form. Despite criticizing a certain type of novel, he acknowledges that fiction has a power over peoples' imaginations that factual data lacks. When Mimi asks Adam how they can persuade people of the validity of their cause he replies, "The best arguments in the world won't change a person's mind. The only thing that can do that is a good story." The author also tackles the thorny issue that may have crossed many peoples' minds while reading *The Overstory* (unless reading it on an e-reader). When the production of books depends upon the felling of trees, is it hypocritical to write a novel condemning deforestation? This point is addressed when Nick works in the fulfilment warehouse of a certain unnamed global company. Disturbed by this face-to-face encounter with mass consumerism, Nick reflects, "The product here is not so much books as … convenience. Ease is the disease …. Once you've bought a novel in your pajamas, there's no turning back." He does, however, find a spark of hope in the assumption that some of those millions of books must be worthy of the paper they are written on. These, presumably, would be books like Patricia Westerford's *The Secret Forest*, Thoreau's *Walden* and Powers's own *The Overstory*—books with the power to change the way people think about trees.

DISCUSSION QUESTIONS

1/ Why is the novel called *The Overstory*? What does the title convey about the author's themes and aims?

2/ Reviewers have sometimes criticized Richard Powers's fiction for prioritizing ideas and themes over characterization. Did you feel that this was an issue in *The Overstory*? Did you find all the characters equally engaging? If not, why not?

3/ Richard Powers admits that, ideally, he would have liked to write *The Overstory* entirely from the perspective of trees. In the end he resisted, feeling that this would be beyond his own "power as a novelist and ... probably ... beyond the imaginative power of identification of most readers." Do you think this is true? Would you choose to read a novel which featured trees as the main characters?

4/ How does the novel contrast human time and tree time (particularly in the story of the successive generations of the Hoel family)?

5/ Discuss the various tree epiphanies experienced by the main characters. Have you ever experienced a similar moment of enlightenment?

6/ Each section of the novel begins with a passage describing an unnamed character as if from a distance (e.g. the description of a woman listening to the conversations of trees). What did you make of these passages? Why does the author choose to use a third-person omniscient narrator in these sections? What effect does it have on the reading experience?

7/ The novel is divided into four sections—"Roots," "Trunk," "Crown," and "Seeds." How do the storylines and themes of each section reflect its title? Did you feel that this narrative structure worked? Which of the four sections did you like best, and why?

8/ At the beginning of the novel, Ray and Dorothy are "two people for whom trees mean almost nothing." How does this change as the story progresses? How does their story relate to the other narratives in the novel?

9/ Discuss the parallels between the goals of Patricia Westerford and those of the author. What challenges do they face in conveying their message? Are they equally successful in their ventures?

10/ Olivia (or Maidenhair as she becomes) has a bewitching effect on the characters she comes into contact with. This impact is enhanced by the fact that she is "gorgeous." Is it necessary for her character to be beautiful? Does this detail undermine the author's representation of a woman as the driving force of environmental protest?

11/ The Brinkmans' marital conflict partially revolves around their inability to have a child. There are also cryptic suggestions, however, that Olivia might be their daughter (e.g. Olivia's father is an intellectual property lawyer, and Dorothy refers to a tattoo on her daughter's shoulder). How did you interpret the section in the novel where Ray and Dorothy discuss planting the chestnut seedling with their daughter? Are these genuine memories, or imaginings? Could Olivia be their real daughter, or is she the child they would have liked to have had?

12/ When Neelay is a child, his father tells him that "Patience is the maker of all good things." How does the novel illustrate the fruits of patience?

13/ There are many religious allusions in *The Overstory*, from references to ancient forms of spirituality to Christian symbolism linking characters to Biblical figures, including Jesus. What did you make of this imagery? What do you think the author hopes to achieve by it?

14/ How does the author relate the psychological phenomenon of "the bystander effect" to the way humans have reacted to large-scale deforestation? Why do you think we find it so difficult to step outside the parameters of social conformity? Have you ever been in an emergency situation and seen the bystander effect in action?

15/ Traditionally, the digital world is often presented as the nemesis of the natural world. In *The Overstory*, however, Powers suggests that this may not necessarily be the case. Discuss the connections the author draws between technology and nature. Do you think it is possible that artificial intelligence could save the planet?

16/ *The Overstory* includes many poetic descriptions of trees. It is also bursting with tree facts and figures. Did any of these images, or nuggets of factual information, particularly stand out for you?

17/ Discuss the way environmental activism is represented in the novel. Do you think the author presents a balanced view of the conflicts between eco-warriors and the logging industry/police force? How did you feel about the characters' progression to eco-terrorism? Do their actions ultimately achieve anything?

18/ Richard Powers makes no secret of the fact that he shares his characters' opposition to deforestation and hopes that his readers will come to share it too. How did you feel about the book's unapologetic ideological message? Does it achieve the effect the author is aiming for? Would you have liked to hear more from characters with an opposing view, for example, the loggers who only appear in cameo roles?

19/ What are Douglas's reasons for betraying Adam to the police? Were you surprised by this plot development? Do you think his decision was in any way justified?

20/ When Patricia gives her speech at an environmental conference, the author ends her narrative with two possibilities. In the first Patricia commits suicide, and in the second she toasts "unsuicide." Which path do you believe she takes, and why?_Is your response based on how you feel about her as a character, or on which course of action would most powerfully convey her message? Do you think human extinction (or suicide) might be the best thing for Earth's future?

21/ Towards the end of his life, Ray Brinkman concludes that trees should be granted the same legal rights as humans. What do you think of this idea?

22/ At the end of the novel Powers offers two glimmers of hope for the planet's future. The first is Patricia's seed bank. The second is the form of artificial intelligence developed by Neelay. Did these possibilities leave you with any sense of optimism?

23/ The author's love of literature is demonstrated in the wide range of texts he refers to in *The Overstory*. At several points, however, his characters critique a certain kind of fiction. How do you feel about the suggestion that character-driven novels are irrelevant to our times? Should literary fiction be tackling bigger subjects than human emotions? Given these arguments, why did Powers choose to write a novel instead of non-fiction?

24/ Nick states, "We need to get smarter about what we need," while Patricia says, "My simple rule of thumb … is this: when you cut down a tree, what you make from it should be at least as miraculous as what you cut down." How did you feel about these philosophies? Do we need to think harder about precisely what the goods we buy are made from, and whether we really need them?

25/ Do you think humans are capable of making the kind of changes that the novel suggests are necessary to save trees and ourselves?

26/ While many critically acclaimed novels have dramatized the potential consequences of ecological disaster (Margaret Atwood's *Oryx and Crake*, Cormac McCarthy's *The Road*, etc.) far fewer have described the decline towards this catastrophe, as *The Overstory* does. Why do you think that is? Should more novelists be tackling this subject?

27/ At just over five hundred pages, *The Overstory* is a hefty work of fiction. Do you think its epic length is justified, or would it have benefited from editing? Were there any narratives or strands of the story that felt unnecessary to you?

28/ When Nick works in a well-known company's fulfilment warehouse, he reflects "Ease is the disease … Once you've bought a novel in your pajamas, there's no turning back." Did you buy your copy of *The Overstory* in the comfort of your own home, perhaps even wearing loungewear? If so, did this passage make you feel guilty?

29/ While working in the fulfilment warehouse, Nick is disturbed by the millions of books stacked on the shelves, thinking of the numerous trees felled to produce them. Is there something essentially problematic in publishing a book condemning deforestation? How do we judge whether a book is worthy of the paper it is written on?

30/ Has reading *The Overstory* made you less "plant-blind"? Has it inspired you to change anything about your own lifestyle—have you planted a tree, created a wild area in your garden, or simply bought less stuff?

31/ Is *The Overstory* a deserving winner of the Pulitzer Prize for Fiction? What are readers' expectations of a Pulitzer prize-winning novel?

32/ In one sentence, sum up your feelings about *The Overstory*.

QUIZ QUESTIONS

1/ Why does the Hoel Chestnut survive when most American chestnuts have died from an imported disease?

2/ How do Nick's parents and grandmother die?

3/ As a teenager, how does Adam keep track of the individuals within an ant colony?

4/ How does Neelay become paralyzed?

5/ How does Mimi's father die?

6/ What do Mimi and her sisters inherit from their father?

7/ Which controversial psychological experiment does Douglas take part in?

8/ Which Shakespearean play do Dorothy and Ray star in when they first meet, and which parts do they play?

9/ What is Ray Brinkman's profession?

10/ What names do Olivia, Nick, Mimi, Douglas and Adam adopt when they become eco-warriors?

11/ What is the name of the Californian redwood tree inhabited by Olivia and Nick?

12/ What name does Neelay give to the hugely addictive computer game he invents?

13/ When Professor Rabinowski has a heart attack, Adam (wrongly) believes he is demonstrating which psychological phenomenon?

14/ As an adult, Adam comes across a copy of his favourite book as a child—*The Golden Guide to Insects*. Who did it once belong to?

15/ At the end of the novel what word does Nick spell out in dead timber?

QUIZ ANSWERS

1/ Jørgen Hoel plants it in Iowa, thousands of miles from its native territory

2/ They are gassed by a propane heater

3/ He paints them with different shades of nail polish

4/ He falls out of an *encina* (Spanish oak) tree

5/ He shoots himself in the head underneath his dying mulberry tree

6/ An ancient Chinese scroll and three jade rings

7/ The Stanford Prison Experiment

8/ They star in *Macbeth*. Dorothy plays Lady Macbeth and Ray is Macduff

9/ He is an intellectual property lawyer

10/ Maidenhair, Watchman, Mulberry, Doug-fir, and Maple

11/ Mimas

12/ *Mastery*

13/ The bystander effect

14/ Ray Brinkman

15/ "STILL"

FURTHER READING

The Echo Maker by Richard Powers

Barkskins by Annie Proulx

Flight Behavior by Barbara Kingsolver

Fox 8 by George Saunders

Cloud Atlas by David Mitchell

New York 2140 by Kim Stanley Robinson

Moby Dick by Herman Melville

The Pearl by John Steinbeck

A Separate Peace by John Knowles

Walden by Henry David Thoreau

My First Summer in the Sierra by John Muir

The Hidden Life of Trees by Peter Wohlleben

The Wild Places by Robert Macfarlane

The Great Derangement: Climate Change and the Unthinkable by Amitav Ghosh

Oak and Ash and Thorn by Peter Fiennes

American Canopy: Trees, Forests, and the Making of a Nation by Eric Rutkow

FURTHER GUIDES IN THIS SERIES

Alias Grace (Margaret Atwood)

Beartown (Fredrik Backman)

Before We Were Yours (Lisa Wingate)

Big Little Lies (Liane Moriarty)

The Book Thief (Markus Zusak)

Circe (Madeline Miller)

Commonwealth (Ann Patchett)

Educated (Tara Westover)

The Fault in Our Stars (John Green)

Frankenstein (Mary Shelley)

A Gentleman in Moscow (Amor Towles)

The Girl on the Train (Paula Hawkins)

Go Set a Watchman (Harper Lee)

A God in Ruins (Kate Atkinson)

The Goldfinch (Donna Tartt)

Gone Girl (Gillian Flynn)

The Great Alone (Kristin Hannah)

The Great Gatsby (F. Scott Fitzgerald)

The Grownup (Gillian Flynn)

The Guernsey Literary and Potato Peel Pie Society (Mary Ann Shaffer & Annie Burrows)

The Heart Goes Last (Margaret Atwood)

The Husband's Secret (Liane Moriarty)

I Know Why the Caged Bird Sings (Maya Angelou)

The Light between Oceans (M.L. Stedman)

Lincoln in the Bardo (George Saunders)

Little Fires Everywhere (Celeste Ng)

My Brilliant Friend (Elena Ferrante)

My Name is Lucy Barton (Elizabeth Strout)

The Narrow Road to the Deep North (Richard Flanagan)

Pachinko (Min Jin Lee)

The Paying Guests (Sarah Waters)

The Secret History (Donna Tartt)

The Storied Life of A.J. Fikry (Gabrielle Zevin)

The Sympathizer (Viet Thanh Nguyen)

The Underground Railroad (Colson Whitehead)

BIBLIOGRAPHY

Richard Powers. *The Overstory*, Vintage, 2019

Katherine Bishop. 'Police Arrest 44 in Redwood Protest.' *The New York Times,* June 21, 1990

India Bourke. 'Richard Powers's eco-novel *The Overstory* urgently challenges our ideas about humanity and nature.' *New Statesman,* August 22, 2018

Ron Charles. 'The most exciting novel about trees you'll ever read.' *The Washington Post*, April 3, 2018

Daniel Green. 'Lost in the Woods: Richard Powers's *The Overstory*.' *Quarterly Conversation*, Issue 52, June 11, 2018

Everett Hamner. 'Here's to Unsuicide: An Interview with Richard Powers.' *Los Angeles Review of Books*, April 7, 2018

Emma John. 'Richard Powers: 'We're completely alienated from everything else alive.' *The Guardian*, June 16, 2018

Sam Jordison. 'Reading Group: How could *The Overstory* be considered a book of the year?' *The Guardian*, December 18, 2018

Peter Kemp. 'Fiction review: The Overstory by Richard Powers.' *The Sunday Times*, April 1, 2018

Barbara Kingsolver. 'The Heroes of This Novel Are Centuries Old and 300 Feet Tall.' *The New York Times*, April 9, 2018

Alexander Larman. '*The Overstory* by Richard Powers review — a majestic redwood of a novel.' *The Guardian*, April 8, 2018

Nathaniel Rich. 'The Novel That Asks, 'What Went Wrong With Mankind?'' The Atlantic, June 2018

David Sexton. '*The Overstory* by Richard Powers - review: slightly barking about the magic of trees.' *Evening Standard*, August 2, 2018

Claire Mive Stanford. 'Speaking for the Trees: Richard Powers's "*The Overstory*." *Los Angeles Review of Books*, May 10, 2018

http://www.richardPowers.net

https://www.prisonexp.org/

https://www.britannica.com/topic/Chipko-movement

https://www.nobelprize.org/prizes/peace/2004/maathai/biographical/

ABOUT THE AUTHOR

Kathryn Cope graduated in English Literature from Manchester University and has a master's degree in contemporary fiction from the University of York. She is the author of Study Guides for Book Clubs and the HarperCollins Official Book Club guides. She lives in the Staffordshire Moorlands with her husband, son and dog.

www.amazon.com/author/kathryncope

Made in the USA
Middletown, DE
08 March 2020